STOC

ACPL ITEM
DISCARDED

650.
Farr
Getting the job you really
want

GETTING THE JOB *You Really* WANT

- Discover your best skills
- Choose the best job (the one you can do well and enjoy)
- Get the job fast
- Get ahead on your new job

J. Michael Farr

JIST Works, Inc.
Indianapolis, Indiana

i

Allen County Public Library
900 Webster Street
PO Box 2270
Fort Wayne, IN 46801-2270

Getting the Job You Really Want
© 1995, JIST Works, Inc.,
Third Edition.

All rights reserved. Printed in the
United States of America. No part
of this book may be reproduced
in any form or by any means, or
stored in a database or retrieval
system, without prior written
permission of the publisher
except in case of brief quotations
embodied in critical articles
or reviews.

Instructor's Guide:
A separate instructor's guide and
other instructional aids are
available from the publisher.
Please contact us for details.

JIST Works, Inc.
720 North Park Avenue
Indianapolis, IN 46202-3431
(317) 264-3720

ISBN 1-56370-092-1

Table of Contents

Introduction

This is the third edition of this book. The earlier editions have been used by about 150 thousand people, so you are in good company in reading it. While I have made a variety of changes in this edition to reflect the recent changes in our economy, the basics of finding and keeping a good job haven't changed all that much.

There are really only two things that are important in planning your career and in looking for a job:

1. If you are going to work, you might as well do something you enjoy and are good at; and,

2. If you need to find a job, you might as well do it in less time.

These topics are what the book is about.

In a very real sense, *Getting the Job You Really Want* is about getting results. It will help you identify a powerful new language to describe your skills and to use that language in interviews.

If you don't have a job objective, it will help you define one. Even if you already know what sort of job you want, you will learn more about it, as well as other jobs that are related. The job search techniques you will learn here have been proven to cut the time it takes to get a job — and will help you get a better job. There is even a chapter on keeping the job once you get it. I have tried to cover all the basic issues you should know about in defining, getting, and keeping a good job.

In may ways, this is more than "just" a job search book. It will encourage you to learn more about yourself. It will help you identify what you enjoy — and are good at — and to include these things in your search for meaningful work. This book is not just about jobs, it is about how you want to live your life. I hope that it helps you make better decisions as well as show you techniques that allow you to be far more effective in your career planning and search for a job.

This is also a book that was designed to be **used** and not just read. Make it your own by writing in it, jotting notes in margins, and completing the activities. I do hope that you enjoy it — and that it helps you get a good job in less time.

I wish you well

Mike Farr

1

Meeting an Employer's Expectations

What the Dickens Do Employers Want?

What does work mean to you? Work can be just a way to earn a living. Something you have to do to eat and have a place to live. Or work can be what you enjoy doing. A way to help you do something you feel is important.

However you feel about work now, your feelings are likely to change during your lifetime.

It's hard to imagine what you will be doing far in the future. But you can be fairly certain that things will change. For example, the U.S. Department of Labor now predicts the average person will change careers five to seven times. And most people change jobs more often than that!

The average 35-year-old has changed jobs once every year and a half since entering the workforce. While you may not change jobs that often, it is very likely that you will change your job many times in your life.

Survival Skills for the Working World

To do well in a competitive and rapidly changing job market, you need a new set of survival skills.

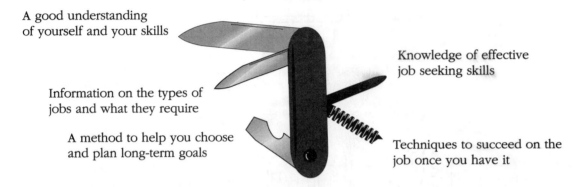

A good understanding of yourself and your skills

Information on the types of jobs and what they require

A method to help you choose and plan long-term goals

Knowledge of effective job seeking skills

Techniques to succeed on the job once you have it

All these topics — and many others — are covered in this book. If you study the information in this book and do the exercises carefully, you will be better prepared for the working world than about 90 percent of all job seekers. You will also be more likely to get and keep the job you want.

An Employer's Expectations

To succeed as a job seeker and worker, you need to understand an employer's point of view. Many people feel that an employer thinks differently than the rest of us. But employers are just like you and me. Try to think like an employer. Consider what you'd want your employees to do and you can figure out what is expected of you as a worker. And knowing what employers want will help you present yourself successfully when you are looking for a job.

Running Your Own Business

Imagine that you run a company. Give your company a name and decide whether you make products or provide a service. Then choose the types of products or services you offer. You can have any kind of company, but it must be fairly large. Next, imagine you have been asked to help others in your company decide which people to hire — or not hire.

Copyright © 1995 • JIST Works, Inc. • Indianapolis, IN 46202 • (317) 264-3720

In the following spaces, see how many reasons you can list that could be used either to screen someone out or to screen someone in for hiring. You can list a negative, such as "sloppy appearance," or a positive, such as "good communication skills." Think of at least ten reasons.

Ten Reasons for Screening In or Out

1. _____
2. _____
3. _____
4. _____
5. _____
6. _____
7. _____
8. _____
9. _____
10. _____

After you have done this, go back and put check marks by the five reasons you think are the most important.

From those five, choose the top three reasons and list them below in order of importance. The most important is number 1.

Your Top Three Reasons

1. _____
2. _____
3. _____

Good work! The reasons you listed are probably like those a real employer would list. Just like you, they will use these reasons *(or ones like them)* to help them decide to hire one person over another. Keep in mind that different employers have different opinions about what is most important. Jobs, too, have different requirements, depending on what that employee will do. That is why different employers might include different things in their own list of things to consider in hiring someone.

Copyright © 1995 • JIST Works, Inc. • Indianapolis, IN 46202 • (317) 264-3720

What Employers Look For

Studies have been made to find out what employers look for in the people they hire. Check your list against the findings of these studies.

> ## In Deciding on Hiring One Person Over Another, Employers Consider:
> Appearance
> Dependability and other personality traits
> Skills, experience, and training

Let's look at why this is true.

Appearance

This is important because a negative first impression is very hard to change. Employers in one survey said that more than 40 percent of the people they interviewed had a poor appearance. They were not dressed or groomed in a way that impressed the interviewer. It may not be fair, but it is a fact.

Did you put appearance on your list?

Why or why not? _____

_____

_____

Dependability

Most employers will not hire someone unless they think that person will be dependable. Being dependable means being on time, having good attendance, and working hard to meet deadlines. It also may mean that you are not likely to leave the job after only a short time. If you convince an employer that you are dependable and hard-working, you will often get the job over an equally skilled person who does not.

How do employers decide who will be dependable? They look at your past experience as well as your present situation. If you have been dependable in the past they know that you are likely to be dependable in the future. The information you provide about previous jobs, school, personal accomplishments, and other

Copyright © 1995 • JIST Works, Inc. • Indianapolis, IN 46202 • (317) 264-3720

history will be very important in helping them decide if you will be dependable. If employers are not convinced that they can depend on you, they will not hire you.

Did you put dependability on your list?

Why or why not? _____

_____

_____

Skills, Experience, and Training

Most employers will interview only those people who have at least the minimum requirements for a job. For example, they would quickly screen out applicants for a secretarial job who could not type or use a word processor. But employers often will hire a person with less training over another applicant. Why? Because they are convinced that person will work harder or be more reliable.

In fact, most decisions are not based only on skills. If the employer thinks you can do the work or that you can quickly learn to do it, he or she may consider you for the job. If the employer thinks you will fit right in, be dependable, and work hard, you may even get the job over someone with more experience than you have!

Did you put skills, experience, and training on your list?

Why or why not? _____

_____

_____

Which lead's me to this conclusion:

Farr's #1 rule of job seeking:

**It is not always the most qualified person
who gets the job — it's the best job seeker!**

Copyright © 1995 • JIST Works, Inc. • Indianapolis, IN 46202 • (317) 264-3720

Employers Are People, Too

Employers are people, just like you. Wouldn't you want to hire people who:

✔ *Look as if they could handle the job,*
✔ *Appear to be good, dependable workers, and*
✔ *Convince you that they have enough job related skills and training to handle the job or could learn quickly?*

This is very good news for you because:

✔ *You can learn to create a positive first impression.*
✔ *You can emphasize why you can be counted on as a dependable worker.*
✔ *You can present your strengths so that you convince an employer that you can do the job. It is often the most prepared job seeker who gets the job, not the best qualified.*

This book will help you prepare. It will help you identify skills you have and enjoy using. It will help you decide what job you can do well and enjoy. And you will learn how to get and succeed on that job, even over more experienced workers.

Copyright © 1995 • JIST Works, Inc. • Indianapolis, IN 46202 • (317) 264-3720

2

Getting the Life You Really Want

There Is More to Life Than Work

Most people work about 40 hours a week — but there are 168 hours in each week! Work takes up only about one-fourth of your time. While it is often an important part of your life, your work is only one part of how you spend your time.

This chapter will help you put work in its place. It will help you define what sort of work you want to do and are likely to be good at. It will also help you define work as part of your life. The ideal job is one that satisfies you. It will help you enjoy what you do for a living, and help you accomplish what you want in life. And this chapter will help you define the ideal job for your work and your life.

Copyright © 1995 • JIST Works, Inc. • Indianapolis, IN 46202 • (317) 264-3720

Preparing for Career Growth

Our economy is changing quickly. No one is sure exactly what this might mean for people who work. As a worker, adapting to changes will become more and more important to your success. For example, *the U. S. Department of Labor estimates that half of all existing jobs will be eliminated or changed in the next 20 years.*

Many of these jobs will be replaced by new ones. People who had held these jobs will have to learn new skills or take new jobs. Those who can't or won't will have to take lower paying jobs or stay unemployed. All this can sound discouraging. But the future holds promise if you can accept change and develop the skills you need.

Millions of new jobs will be created in the years to come. There will be enough new jobs created to replace the ones that were lost, plus many millions of new jobs. Many of these new jobs will require different skills and training than those of the past. There will be many new opportunities for those who are prepared to accept them.

To prepare for the future, you need to think about more than just the type of job you want. You need to consider what is important to you. *The better you understand yourself, the more successfully you can plan your future.* This will help you make better plans for additional training or education, and for your career and your life.

 Each of the following exercises will give you different information about yourself. This will help you make better career and life plans as you use the rest of this book.

Copyright © 1995 • JIST Works, Inc. • Indianapolis, IN 46202 • (317) 264-3720

What Do You Want to Be Doing in Ten Years?

Directions: *Imagine yourself ten years from now. If you could choose exactly what your life would be like, what would you be doing? Be realistic but positive — it's OK to dream! Take your time and answer the following questions. Use extra sheets of paper as needed.*

1. Where would you be living, in what sort of area, in what sort of home? _____
_____
_____
_____
_____
_____

2. How would you be making a living, doing what sorts of things? _____
_____
_____
_____
_____
_____

3. Who *(or with what sorts of people)* would you be sharing your time with? _____
_____
_____
_____
_____

4. How would you spend your leisure time, doing what sorts of things? _____
_____
_____
_____
_____

Copyright © 1995 • JIST Works, Inc. • Indianapolis, IN 46202 • (317) 264-3720

5. Any other important details? _____

_____

_____

_____

_____

An Inheritance from Uncle Harry

Let's imagine you just inherited twenty million dollars from an uncle you didn't even know you had. If you didn't want to, you would never have to work again. But there are a few catches! Harry put the money with a group of bankers. And these people will give the money to you only after you have met certain conditions. Answer the following questions as honestly as you can.

1. For two years, you will get $75,000 per year for expenses. You can do anything you want, but you must spend your time learning about something that interests you. How would you spend this time, doing what sorts of things?

_____

_____

_____

_____

_____

2. After two years, you must spend half of your money *(ten million dollars!)* on a project that would help others. What would this project be?_____

_____

_____

_____

_____

10

Copyright © 1995 • JIST Works, Inc. • Indianapolis, IN 46202 • (317) 264-3720

3. What sort of lifestyle would you have after the two years were over? Where would you live, with whom, and how would you spend your time? _____

_____

_____

_____

_____

What Do You Want to Accomplish?

Ten years from now, what are the three things you would like to have accomplished? Don't think of all the reasons you might not succeed. Concentrate on the things you really would like to accomplish.

1. _____

_____

_____

2. _____

_____

_____

3. _____

_____

_____

You Can Make Your Wishes Come True

The activities you just finished help you think about the future. They allow you to think about what you really want to do or accomplish. These "dreams" can also give you ideas about what you really want to do in your work and your life.

While you may not be able to do everything that you want, good planning can help you get closer. What can you do now to start making your dreams come true?

Copyright © 1995 • JIST Works, Inc. • Indianapolis, IN 46202 • (317) 264-3720

Take action! Be clear about your goals and set up something you can do to meet them. The activities that follow (and throughout this book) will help you move closer to your dreams. The rest, of course, will be up to you.

Setting Goals

 Look over the exercises you've just completed. Pick the three achievements or goals that seem most important to you and write them here. Be realistic about what you could accomplish if you worked at it. Think in terms of ten years into the future.

Goal 1._____

Goal 2._____

Goal 3._____

For each of these goals, complete the following.

Goal 1: _____

1. Give details about this goal. What you would like to accomplish?

   _____

   _____

   _____

   _____

   _____

   _____

2. Within the next two years, what three things could you do to move closer to this goal?

   a. _____

   _____

   b. _____

   _____

   c. _____

   _____

Copyright © 1995 • JIST Works, Inc. • Indianapolis, IN 46202 • (317) 264-3720

3. List at least three things you could do in the next six months to begin working toward this goal.

a. _____

_____

_____

b. _____

_____

_____

c. _____

_____

_____

4. List at least three things you could do in the next 30 days to begin working toward this goal.

a. _____

_____

_____

b. _____

_____

_____

c. _____

_____

_____

Goal 2: _____

1. Give details about this goal. What you would like to accomplish?

_____

_____

_____

_____

_____

_____

Copyright © 1995 • JIST Works, Inc. • Indianapolis, IN 46202 • (317) 264-3720

2. Within the next two years, what three things could you do to move closer to this goal?

   a. _____
      _____
      _____

   b. _____
      _____
      _____

   c. _____
      _____
      _____

3. List at least three things you could do in the next six months to begin working toward this goal.

   a. _____
      _____
      _____

   b. _____
      _____
      _____

   c. _____
      _____
      _____

4. List at least three things you could do in the next 30 days to begin working toward this goal.

   a. _____
      _____
      _____

   b. _____
      _____
      _____

   c. _____
      _____
      _____

14

Copyright © 1995 • JIST Works, Inc. • Indianapolis, IN 46202 • (317) 264-3720

Goal 3: _____

1. Give details about this goal. What you would like to accomplish?

   _____
   _____
   _____
   _____
   _____
   _____
   _____
   _____

2. Within the next two years, what three things could you do to move closer to this goal?

   a. _____
      _____

   b. _____
      _____

   c. _____
      _____

3. List at least three things you could do in the next six months to begin working toward this goal.

   a. _____
      _____

   b. _____
      _____

   c. _____
      _____

Copyright © 1995 • JIST Works, Inc. • Indianapolis, IN 46202 • (317) 264-3720

4. List at least three things you could do in the next 30 days to begin working toward this goal.

a. _____

_____

_____

b. _____

_____

_____

c. _____

_____

_____

Dreams Can Come True
If You Are Willing to Work at Them

Dreaming is not enough. While you could get lucky, planning to meet your goals is a far more effective way to get what you want from life. This chapter has helped you to consider some of your long-term goals. You can often find ways to include these goals in your career planning. Then you can create a more meaningful and enjoyable future for yourself.

Copyright © 1995 • JIST Works, Inc. • Indianapolis, IN 46202 • (317) 264-3720

3

What Are You Good At?

Developing Your Skills Language

You have hundreds of skills. Most people do, yet very few are able to explain their skills to others. You may take for granted many things you do well that others would find hard or even impossible to do.

One study of employers found that three out of every four people interviewed for a job did not present the skills they had to do the job. Most people just don't have the language to present the skills they have.

In planning your career or in looking for a job, knowing what you can do well is very important. It can help you decide what kind of work is right for you. It makes a lot of sense to do the things you do best. If you do, you will probably be more successful.

It is also important to do things you enjoy doing. If you enjoy what you do and are good at it, your job and your life will be more satisfying.

This chapter provides a series of exercises to help you identify what you are good at and enjoy doing. It will help you develop a powerful "skills language" that can help you in planning your career and, later, in getting a good job.

The Three Types of Skills

Although you have hundreds of skills, you may find it hard to name them. One way to define your skills is to organize them into three groups:

Each of us have hundreds of skills, divided into these three types:

Job-Related Skills

These are skills you need for a specific job. An auto mechanic, for example, needs to know how to tune engines, repair brakes, and use a variety of tools. He or she also needs to have other skills related to auto repairs. Most people think of jobs skills when they are asked what skills they have. While these skills are important, there are other skills that also are important for you to know.

Adaptive Skills

These skills also can be defined as personality traits or personal characteristics. They help a person adapt to or get along in a new situation. For example, honesty and enthusiasm are traits employers look for in a good worker. While many job seekers do not emphasize these skills in an interview, they are very important to employers.

Transferable Skills

These are skills you can use in many different jobs. They can transfer from one job to a very different one. Writing clearly or the ability to organize things are two examples of transferable skills you can use in almost any job.

Copyright © 1995 • JIST Works, Inc. • Indianapolis, IN 46202 • (317) 264-3720

It is important to know what skills you have. Most job seekers think job-related skills are their most important skills. They are important. But employers often select job seekers with less experience who present their adaptive and transferable skills well in an interview. For this reason, knowing and being able to describe your skills can often give you a big advantage in getting the job you want.

Discover Your Adaptive Skills

 In the space that follows, list five things about yourself that you think make you a good worker. Take your time. Think about what an employer might like about you or the way you work.

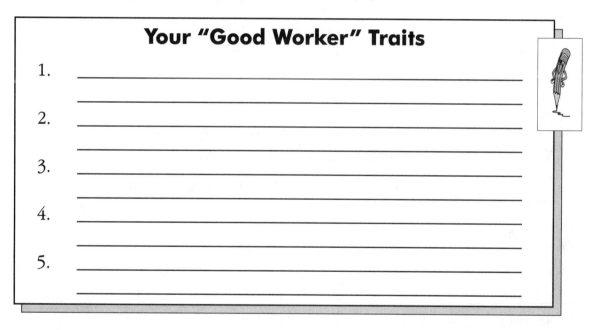

Your "Good Worker" Traits

1. _____

2. _____

3. _____

4. _____

5. _____

If you were an employer, would these skills be important for you to know about? Would knowing job seekers' adaptive skills help you decide to hire one person over another?

In most cases, it would. Yet many people do not even mention their adaptive skills in an interview! Use the checklist that follows to learn more about the adaptive skills you have.

Copyright © 1995 • JIST Works, Inc. • Indianapolis, IN 46202 • (317) 264-3720

Adaptive Skills Checklist

Directions: *You may have overlooked some important adaptive skills. The following checklist shows skills most employers find important. Read each skill carefully. If you have or use that skill some of the time, put a check mark in the first column. If you have or use that skill most of the time, go ahead and put a check mark in the second column. Don't mark either column if you don't use that skill very often.*

Critical Skills

These are skills all employers value highly. They often won't hire a person who does not have or use some of these.

EMPLOYERS VALUE PEOPLE WHO:

Skills	Most of the time	Some of the time	Skills	Most of the time	Some of the time
get to work every day			get along well with coworkers		
arrive on time			are honest		
get things done			work hard		
follow instructions from supervisor					

Other Adaptive Skills

GOOD WORKERS HAVE THE FOLLOWING ADAPTIVE SKILLS:

Skills	Most of the time	Some of the time	Skills	Most of the time	Some of the time
ambition			intelligence		
patience			creativity		
assertiveness			leadership		
learn quickly			enthusiasm		
flexibility			persistence		
maturity			self-motivation		
dependability			are results-oriented		
complete assignments			pride in doing a good job		
sincerity			willingness to learn new things		
solve problems			take responsibility		
friendliness			ask questions		
good sense of humor			other:		
physical strength					
good sense of direction					
highly motivated					

Copyright © 1995 • JIST Works, Inc. • Indianapolis, IN 46202 • (317) 264-3720

Use the blank lines at the end of the list to add other adaptive skills that are important to you but that were not listed. Include any from the list of Your Good Worker Traits you completed earlier in this section.

Your Top Adaptive Skills

Review the Adaptive Skills Checklist carefully. Select the three skills you checked in column 1 that you think are most important to an employer. List these skills below.

REMEMBER

Your Top Three Adaptive Skills

1. _____
2. _____
3. _____

Save This List!

It can be very important to you! These are the adaptive skills or personality traits you should emphasize in job interviews. For you, these are some of the most important words in this book! Employers will find them very important in deciding to hire you over someone else. *In chapters 8, 9, and 10 you will learn how mentioning these traits will help you in your job search.*

Discover Your Transferable Skills

Remember that transferable skills can be transferred from one job to another. You have *hundreds* of these skills. They have been learned and used at home, in school, hobbies, leisure activities, previous volunteer and paid jobs, and in many other activities.

The Transferable Skills Checklist that follows will help you identify some of these skills. It includes skills that are important to employers and job success.

Transferable Skills Checklist

Directions: *Review each entry carefully. If you have a skill and are good at it, put a check mark in the first column. If you want to use that same skill in your next job, put a check mark in the second column. Add*

any other skills you want to include in the "other" section. When you're finished, you should have checked ten to twenty skills in both columns.

Critical Skills

These skills tend to get you higher levels of responsibility and pay. They are worth emphasizing in an interview! If you have these transferable skills you are able to:

Skills	Strong Skill	Next Job	Skills	Strong Skill	Next Job
meet deadlines			solve problems		
speak in public			plan		
supervise others			understand and control budgets		
accept responsibility			increase sales or efficiency		

Other Transferable Skills

KEY SKILLS

Skills	Strong Skill	Next Job	Skills	Strong Skill	Next Job
instruct others			negotiate		
manage money			organize/manage projects		
manage people			speak in public		
meet deadlines			write well		
meet the public					

USING MY HANDS/DEALING WITH THINGS

Skills	Strong Skill	Next Job	Skills	Strong Skill	Next Job
assemble things			observe/inspect		
build things			operate tools		
construct/repair buildings			repair things		
drive, operate vehicles			use complex equipment		
am good with hands					

DEALING WITH DATA

Skills	Strong Skill	Next Job	Skills	Strong Skill	Next Job
analyze data			count		
audit records			detail-oriented		
set up budgets			evaluate		
calculate/compute			investigate		
check for accuracy			keep financial records		
classify things			locate answers, information		
compare			manage money		
compile			observe/inspect		

Copyright © 1995 • JIST Works, Inc. • Indianapolis, IN 46202 • (317) 264-3720

Other Transferable Skills *(Continued)*

DEALING WITH DATA *(Continued)*

Skills	Strong Skill	Next Job	Skills	Strong Skill	Next Job
record facts			synthesize		
research			take inventory		

WORKING WITH PEOPLE

Skills	Strong Skill	Next Job	Skills	Strong Skill	Next Job
administer			outgoing		
care for			patience		
confront others			persuade		
counsel people			pleasant		
demonstrate			sensitive		
diplomatic			sociable		
help others			supervise		
have insight			tactful		
instruct			teaching		
interview people			tolerant		
kind			tough		
listen			trusting		
mentor			understanding		
negotiate					

USING WORDS, IDEAS

Skills	Strong Skill	Next Job	Skills	Strong Skill	Next Job
articulate			inventive		
communicate verbally			library research		
correspond with others			logical		
create new ideas			public speaking		
design			remembering information		
edit			write clearly		
ingenious					

LEADERSHIP

Skills	Strong Skill	Next Job	Skills	Strong Skill	Next Job
arrange social functions			direct others		
competitive			explain things to others		
decisive			influence others		
delegate			initiate new tasks		

Copyright © 1995 • JIST Works, Inc. • Indianapolis, IN 46202 • (317) 264-3720

Other Transferable Skills *(Continued)*

LEADERSHIP *(Continued)*

Skills	Strong Skill	Next Job	Skills	Strong Skill	Next Job
make decisions			results oriented		
manage or direct others			take risks		
mediate problems			run meetings		
motivate people			self-confident		
negotiate agreements			self-motivated		
planning			solve problems		

CREATIVE/ARTISTIC

Skills	Strong Skill	Next Job	Skills	Strong Skill	Next Job
artistic			perform, act		
draw			present artistic ideas		
paint			dance, body movement		
expressive					

OTHERS:

Skills	Strong Skill	Next Job	Skills	Strong Skill	Next Job

Your Top Transferable Skills

Carefully review your list of transferable skills. Then select the top five skills you want to use in your next job and list them below.

REMEMBER

Your Top Five Transferable Skills

1. _____
2. _____
3. _____
4. _____
5. _____

Copyright © 1995 • JIST Works, Inc. • Indianapolis, IN 46202 • (317) 264-3720

Your Power Skills

Over the years, you have done things that have given you a great sense of accomplishment. These could be something you did long ago — or yesterday — that wouldn't mean much to anyone else. Perhaps it was that first bike ride you made all by yourself. Or the delicious bread you baked last week. Or that award you got in grade school. You may or may not have gotten any recognition for what you did. But you did it well and enjoyed doing it.

The things you remember as accomplishments can be another source for discovering your skills. For example, riding a bike requires working by yourself, not giving up, and taking chances. To bake bread you need to follow directions, organize and measure ingredients, and work with your hands.

Skills that you use in your special accomplishments are *power skills.* These are skills that you are good at and enjoy using. They can be any type of skill including adaptive, transferable, or job-related skills. If you can identify them — and use them in your next job — you will have a much better chance of success and satisfaction in your career.

List Your Accomplishments

To help identify your power skills, complete the following exercises.

1. List three accomplishments from the years before high school that are important to you.

    a. _____

    _____

    _____

    b. _____

    _____

    _____

    c. _____

    _____

    _____

2. List three accomplishments from your high school years.

   a. _____

   _____

   _____

   b. _____

   _____

   _____

   c. _____

   _____

   _____

3. List three accomplishments from your adult years.

   a. _____

   _____

   _____

   b. _____

   _____

   _____

   c. _____

   _____

   _____

Write a Story for Your Accomplishments

Select one accomplishment from each of the above groups. Select those that mean the most to you, ones you truly enjoyed doing. Write a detailed story about each accomplishment on the following lines. Use your own paper if you need more space.

Story 1

_____

_____

_____

Copyright © 1995 • JIST Works, Inc. • Indianapolis, IN 46202 • (317) 264-3720

Story 1 (Continued)

_____
_____
_____
_____
_____
_____
_____
_____

Story 2

_____
_____
_____
_____
_____
_____
_____
_____
_____
_____
_____
_____
_____

Story 3

_____
_____
_____
_____
_____
_____
_____
_____
_____
_____
_____
_____

Copyright © 1995 • JIST Works, Inc. • Indianapolis, IN 46202 • (317) 264-3720

Accomplishments to Skills

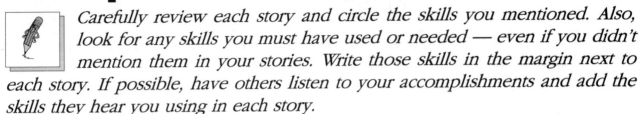

Carefully review each story and circle the skills you mentioned. Also, look for any skills you must have used or needed — even if you didn't mention them in your stories. Write those skills in the margin next to each story. If possible, have others listen to your accomplishments and add the skills they hear you using in each story.

When you are done, list all the skills from the three stories in the spaces that follow. Put a check mark by those skills that are mentioned in more than one story.

Some Skills You Used in Your Accomplishments

Identifying Your Power Skills

Now review the lists of top adaptive and transferable skills that you completed earlier. If any of those skills are not on the list you just made, add them now. From this combined list, select the five skills you would most enjoy using in your next job. List those five skills, in their order of importance to you, in the spaces that follow.

Copyright © 1995 • JIST Works, Inc. • Indianapolis, IN 46202 • (317) 264-3720

REMEMBER

Your Top Five Power Skills

1. _____
2. _____
3. _____
4. _____
5. _____

These are your *power skills.* You are likely to enjoy and do well in a job that allows you to use all or most of these skills. Along with your lists of top skills that you completed earlier, it is important for you to look for jobs that allow you to use these skills. And, as mentioned before, mentioning your key skills in an interview can often help you get jobs over those with better credentials.

4

Planning Your Career and Setting a Job Objective

A Career Is Not Just a Job

A job is something you do to earn money. A *career* is different. When you choose to do a certain type of work, you are making a career decision. Even if you change jobs, you can often continue in the same career area. For example, someone who chooses a career in banking (an industry) or teaching (an occupation) will tend to stay in banking or teaching, even if that person changes jobs.

Many people simply take a job and, as they gain experience, decide to stay in that field. They look for new jobs based on what they have learned and done in the past. Without really thinking much about it, one job leads to another. Over time, this often becomes a career choice. While this approach sometimes works out, it is not the best way to go about such an important task.

This chapter will help you make better decisions about what jobs most interest you. The best approach to selecting a job is to consider it as a *career* decision. One job can become a stepping stone to another. The skills you learn in one job can help you succeed in another. If you choose your jobs wisely, you are actually making career decisions.

In making these decisions, consider what you have learned in earlier chapters. Look for jobs that use skills that you are good at and enjoy using. Your career decisions should also include other things that are important to you such as what you want to accomplish in life. Remember that this is not just a decision about a job, you are making decisions about your *career.*

Selecting a Job Objective

The U.S. Department of Labor tracks more than 12,000 job titles. That is entirely too many for you to seriously consider. Fortunately, most people work in just a few hundred major occupations. Information on each of these is provided later in this chapter. Because they are arranged in clusters of similar jobs, you can quickly find those jobs that most interest you.

Even if you already have a good idea of the type of job you want, you can still benefit from this chapter. That is because there are many jobs that you probably haven't considered. Many jobs that use similar skills are in different industries and fields or have different job titles. Good jobs can't even be considered unless you know they exist.

So this chapter helps you decide what types of jobs interest you most. If you already have a good idea about the job you want, this chapter will also help you learn more about it.

Choosing Your Career

Choosing the right career is not easy. Many people make mistakes. They may even get additional education or training only to find out later that they don't like the career they prepared for. Many others simply take the first job they're offered. Sometimes it works out, but often it does not.

This chapter will help you in several ways:

By Looking at Your Interests

You probably have some idea of the kinds of jobs that interest you. These are often jobs you could do well. Even if you need more training or education, it is often worth doing what interests you most.

By Matching What You Want with What the Job Offers

You don't always know what working in a particular job is really like so you need to define what you want in a job. Then you can see how various jobs match up. This allows you to select jobs that are most likely to satisfy you as long-term careers.

Copyright © 1995 • JIST Works, Inc. • Indianapolis, IN 46202 • (317) 264-3720

By Learning about Job Titles and Similar Occupations

There are many jobs you may not consider because you don't know much about them. This chapter introduces you to new job titles and gives you information on them.

By Knowing Sources of Additional Information

This chapter contains information on hundreds of job titles. Once you've decided which jobs interest you, it's worth your time to learn even more about them. You will learn how to find out more about the jobs that interest you.

There are many things to consider in exploring career and job alternatives.

Career Exploration Activities

Several checklists and other activities follow to help you consider important things such as interests, leisure activities, educational requirements, and other factors.

Later in this chapter you will find a listing of jobs along with information about each one. The list is called the Job Matching Chart. Completing the activities that follow will also help you use the Job Matching Chart to select careers that most closely match your interests.

Education and Training Worksheet

Are you willing to get additional training or education? There are always exceptions, but the better jobs often require special training or education.

 Directions: *Check the highest level of training or education you would be willing to get for the job you want. For now, don't worry about how you would pay for this.*

High School Diploma (H)	For jobs requiring a high school education or GED (General Education Diploma) certificate.
Post Secondary Training (P)	Requires training and/or education beyond high school but less than a 4-year college degree. This might include formal on-the-job training; completing an apprenticeship program; attending technical or vocational school; or going to a business, junior, or community college. Can include completing a 2-year associate's degree or shorter programs.
4-Year College and Above (C)	Requires at least a bachelor's degree. If going to college full time, this would typically require four years of full-time study, although special programs can reduce this time requirement. Some jobs, such as attorney and physician, require education and training beyond the bachelor's degree.

Copyright © 1995 • JIST Works, Inc. • Indianapolis, IN 46202 • (317) 264-3720

Note: *The Job Matching Chart uses the H, P and C codes given previously. When no educational level is indicated, that occupation may be entered with less than a high school education. In some cases, the Chart indicates more than one level of education can be used for entry into that occupation. For example, some high school graduates become administrative services managers by being promoted within an organization. Even though more education may not be required in these jobs, it usually improves the chances of being hired and promoted. Education requirements may also vary within an occupation. For example, registered nursing can be entered by earning a diploma, associate's degree, or bachelor's degree.*

Job Requirements and Skills Worksheet

One way to narrow down the jobs to consider is to look at what they require. All jobs require skills and qualities related to data, to people, and to things. Specific skills within each of these groupings are presented below, along with examples of how these skills would be used in various jobs.

 Directions: *Review each skill carefully, then check the **Yes** column if you want or are willing to accept this skill or requirement in your next job. Check the **No** column if you don't. If it is not important to you either way, check the* ***Not Sure*** *column.*

SKILL OR JOB REQUIREMENT	TYPICAL ACTIVITIES	YES	NO	NOT SURE
Skills Related to Working with Information and Data				
Researching and Compiling: Gathering and organizing information or data by reading, conducting tests or experiments, or interviewing experts.	Through research, scientists gather information to develop new theories, products, and processes, such as a new medicine to cure a disease. Paralegals conduct research and compile information to identify appropriate laws, legal articles, and judicial decisions that might be used in a client's case. Credit clerks and authorizers compile and update information for credit reports			
Analyzing and Evaluating: Examining data or information to develop conclusions or interpretations.	After conducting research and compiling data, paralegals may analyze the information and write reports that are used by attorneys to decide how a case should be handled. Retail buyers study sales data to determine purchasing trends, and budget analysts examine financial data to determine the most efficient distribution of funds and resources for their company.			

 Copyright © 1995 • JIST Works, Inc. • Indianapolis, IN 46202 • (317) 264-3720

SKILL OR JOB REQUIREMENT	TYPICAL ACTIVITIES	YES	NO	NOT SURE
Troubleshooting: Identifying, diagnosing, and solving problems. A degree of analysis may be required to form opinions and make decisions. Involves a reaction to a situation or problem that arises.	Elevator repairers diagnose and repair electrical defects quickly to ensure that elevators continue running smoothly. Automotive mechanics diagnose problems with cars and make adjustments or repairs. Managers must deal with various problems, such as a decline in an employee's performance or budget reductions requiring layoffs.			
Artistic Expression: Designing, composing, drawing, writing, or creating original works or concepts.	Interior designers need creativity to develop drawings and specifications for interior construction of buildings. They need an artistic sense to coordinate colors, select furniture and floor coverings, and design lighting and architectural details. Newspaper columnists convey their views on political, social, and economic issues.			

Skills Related to Working with People

SKILL OR JOB REQUIREMENT	TYPICAL ACTIVITIES	YES	NO	NOT SURE
Instructing: Teaching people by explaining or showing. Often requires ability to develop new methods and approaches.	Adult education teachers demonstrate various techniques to students, including the use of tools or equipment. Manufacturers and wholesale sales representatives show their customers how to operate and maintain new equipment.			
Treating and Advising: Counseling or caring for others.	Dietitians advise people on proper nutrition. Psychologists and counselors help people deal with work and marital problems. Securities and financial services sales representatives advise people on financial investments and planning.			
Supervising: Directing, organizing, and motivating people and groups.	Blue-collar worker supervisors coordinate and supervise the activities of subordinates. Education administrators provide direction, leadership, and day-to-day management of educational activities in schools and instructional organizations in private businesses.			
Persuading: Influencing the feelings of others. Preaching, selling, promoting, speechmaking, negotiating, and mediating are among the skills included with this occupational characteristic.	Lawyers attempt to persuade a jury to believe a client's case. Advertising executives try to influence consumers to buy the products they are promoting.			
Public Contact: Meeting, assisting, and dealing directly with the public, frequently on a daily basis.	Reference librarians work directly with people helping them locate information. Bank tellers cash checks and process deposits and withdrawals for customers. Real estate agents help customers find homes that meet their needs.			

Skills Related to Working with Things

SKILL OR JOB REQUIREMENT	TYPICAL ACTIVITIES	YES	NO	NOT SURE
Mechanical Ability: Using and understanding machines or tools extensively. Setting up, operating, adjusting, and repairing machines may also be required.	Textile machinery operators make minor repairs and restart looms when malfunctions occur. Musical instrument repairers tune and adjust pianos and other instruments. Marine engineers maintain and repair engines, boilers, generators, and other machinery on boats and ships.			

SKILL OR JOB REQUIREMENT	TYPICAL ACTIVITIES	YES	NO	NOT SURE
Operating a Vehicle: Driving and controlling vehicles or equipment.	Bus drivers, industrial truck operators, and aircraft pilots are several examples.			

My Top Three Skills or Job Requirements

Review the worksheet you just completed and select the three skills or job requirements that you feel are most important to include in planning your career. List them below, beginning with the most important one.

1. _____
2. _____
3. _____

Preferred Working Conditions Worksheet

The Job Matching Chart presented later includes information on working conditions found in various jobs. Most jobs will have one or more things about it that you may not like. For example, office workers may have to work in confined areas and do repetitive work. Computer operators may have to work some nights and weekends. Agricultural workers must work outside in extreme weather conditions. Since no job is perfect, don't exclude a job simply because it has one or more undesirable elements.

Directions: *Look over the various working conditions that follow then check the **Yes** column if you prefer or are willing to accept this working condition in your next job. Check the **No** column if you don't. If that working condition is not important to you either way, check the **Not Important** column.*

WORKING CONDITIONS	YES	NO	NOT IMPORTANT
Repetitious: Work in which the same duties are performed continuously. Sometimes a machine sets the pace of work. Examples include workers on automotive assembly lines, as well as cashiers and bank tellers.			
Geographically Concentrated: Occupations concentrated in a particular region or locality. For example, most textile workers are concentrated in a few regions. Advertising workers are found mostly in large cities.			

Copyright © 1995 • JIST Works, Inc. • Indianapolis, IN 46202 • (317) 264-3720

WORKING CONDITIONS	YES	NO	NOT IMPORTANT
Mobile: Requires frequent movement between various work locations, such as office buildings and construction sites. Can involve a variety of different work settings. Workers do not stay in a single office, factory or laboratory. For example, in addition to working in an office, property and real estate managers frequently visit properties they oversee, while manufacturing sales representatives travel to different cities to visit customers. Messengers deliver packages to various locations.			
Physical Stamina: Physically demanding. Workers must endure significant physical stress and strain, including lifting heavy objects. Construction work is often strenuous and workers spend most of the day on their feet — bending, kneeling, lifting, and maneuvering heavy objects.			
Part Time: Opportunities for part-time work are favorable. Most waiters and waitresses work part time, as do retail sales workers.			
Irregular Hours: Working a schedule other than the standard 8-hour day, including night or weekend shifts, rotating schedules, or working for several days and then having several days off. Many nurses and security guards work nights or weekends. Other occupations that work on shifts include firefighters, pilots, and factory workers.			

Review Your Interests and Experiences

Things that interest you now or from the past are a good source of ideas for jobs that might interest you in the future. The worksheets that follow help you look at four important sources of your interests — people you know, leisure activities, school subjects, and previous work experiences. Complete each worksheet as well as you can. Later, this information will help you identify jobs on the Job Matching Chart.

People You Know and Related Jobs Worksheet

People you know and the work they do effect your own ideas about jobs. Some of those jobs may seem interesting to you and others are not. Even if you don't know much about these jobs, they can help you discover what interests you.

 Directions: *Think of three jobs that seem interesting to you and are held by people you know. Write those jobs below. For each, briefly describe what you like about that job.*

JOBS HELD BY PEOPLE I KNOW	THINGS I LIKE ABOUT THIS JOB
Job 1: _____	_____ _____ _____ _____

Copyright © 1995 • JIST Works, Inc. • Indianapolis, IN 46202 • (317) 264-3720

JOBS HELD BY PEOPLE I KNOW	THINGS I LIKE ABOUT THIS JOB
Job 2: _____	_____ _____ _____ _____
Job 3: _____	_____ _____ _____ _____

Leisure Activities and Related Jobs Worksheet

How do you like to spend your free time? What interests you? What do you know a lot about? Do you have any hobbies? Your favorite free-time activities could provide some clues to jobs that might interest you.

 Directions: *In the spaces below, list activities that you enjoy doing in your leisure time. Next to each, list any jobs that might be related to that activity. For example, if you like to watch sports, perhaps you could sell sports equipment, coach, do live coverage for sports events, or even work for a sports-related organization.*

LEISURE ACTIVITY	RELATED JOBS
1: _____	_____ _____ _____
2: _____	_____ _____ _____
3: _____	_____ _____ _____

Copyright © 1995 • JIST Works, Inc. • Indianapolis, IN 46202 • (317) 264-3720

School Subjects and Related Jobs Worksheet

Courses you take in school can often give you ideas about occupations that interest you. Even subjects that interested you but that you did not do well in should be considered.

Directions: *This worksheet organizes courses and occupations within major groupings. Put a check mark next to any major grouping of subjects that interests you on the left. Then, circle any subjects or occupations in the right column that seem particularly interesting to you. Note that there are many other jobs and courses that are not included. You can write in any additional jobs that could relate to a subject area that interests you.*

MAJOR GROUP	SUBJECTS OR OCCUPATIONS
___ Agriculture	forestry, agricultural management, animal science, farming, fishery, horticulture, landscaping occupations, agriculture mechanics
___ Art	art education, commercial art, design occupations, drawing, graphic arts, interior decorating, painting, performing arts (such as dancing or acting), sculpture, and communication occupations (such as writing)
___ Business Administration and Finance	accounting, business administration, business finance, business law, economics, business education, business math, entrepreneurial/self-employment studies
___ Distributive Education	marketing, merchandising, sales, retail management
___ Driver Education	transportation occupations, driver education
___ Health	first aid, health education, medical or dental technology, nursing, research
___ Home Economics	child care, clothing and textiles, cosmetology/beauty care, fashion design, food management, food preparation (cooking, baking), sewing and tailoring, home or institutional management

Copyright © 1995 • JIST Works, Inc. • Indianapolis, IN 46202 • (317) 264-3720

MAJOR GROUP	SUBJECTS OR OCCUPATIONS
___ Industrial Arts/Shop	auto body repair, auto mechanics, carpentry, construction; heating, air conditioning, refrigeration; industrial production; mechanical and repairing occupations (such as auto or office machine repair); office equipment or computer repair; plumbing; print shop; small appliance repair
___ Language Arts	communications, English language skills, foreign languages, journalism, literature, speech
___ Mathematics	scientific and technical occupations, social science occupations, engineering, teaching math, statistics
___ Music	education occupations, performing arts, instrumental and vocal music
___ Office Procedures	Bookkeeping, data processing, computer operations, stenography, word processing
___ Physical Education	teaching, health occupations, coaching
___ Science	biology, chemistry, earth or space science, medicine, physics, physiology, zoology
___ Social Studies	Geography, government or political science, psychology, sociology, education occupations, social science, social service
___ Technical Studies	computer programming, computer repair, drafting, electronics, mechanical drawing, surveying
___ Theater Arts	dance, drama, stage craft

Copyright © 1995 • JIST Works, Inc. • Indianapolis, IN 46202 • (317) 264-3720

Previous Work Experience and Related Jobs Worksheet

Jobs you have held in the past can often teach you about what you do or do not want to do in the future.

Directions: *List three past jobs below. In the second column, list things that you did and did not like about each one.*

JOBS HELD	THINGS I DID/DID NOT LIKE ABOUT THIS JOB
Job 1: _____	Likes: _____ _____ _____ Dislikes: _____ _____
Job 2: _____	Likes: _____ _____ _____ Dislikes: _____ _____
Job 3: _____	Likes: _____ _____ _____ Dislikes: _____ _____

Copyright © 1995 • JIST Works, Inc. • Indianapolis, IN 46202 • (317) 264-3720

Top Interests and Experiences

Directions: *Review the worksheets you just completed. These worksheets helped you look at job options based on people you know, leisure activities, school subjects, and previous work experiences. Select the three things from these worksheets that seem most important for you to consider in future career decision making. List them below, in their order of importance to you.*

1. _____
2. _____
3. _____

Using the Job Matching Chart

The Job Matching Chart provides information on about 200 jobs. These are the most popular jobs in our economy, employing about 80 percent of all workers.

The jobs are organized into clusters of similar jobs. This allows you to identify major areas of interest and to consider a variety of jobs within that cluster. Review each cluster so that you can consider jobs you may have previously overlooked. If a job interests you, put a checkmark by that job. After you have looked at the entire chart, go back and review the jobs that you checked more carefully. Circle those jobs that interest you most. These jobs will be worth learning more about.

The information in the Chart are estimates and projections. They may not apply to a particular job or jobs in your region. Working conditions, skills required, pay, and other factors can vary greatly from one "similar" job to another. Projections for the future sometimes do not come true, or are very different from the conditions in your region.

Codes Used in the Job Matching Chart

Following are the education codes used in the Chart.

Code	Description
H	High School Diploma
P	Post Secondary Training (training or education beyond high school)
C	4-year College Degree and Above (post college education that leads to a master's degree, doctorate, or other)
—	Typically learned on the job or no formal training typically available

Copyright © 1995 • JIST Works, Inc. • Indianapolis, IN 46202 • (317) 264-3720

Code	Future Growth Column	Earnings Column
VL	**Very Low:** within the lowest 20% of all occupations	$15 to $20,000/yr.
L	**Low:** within the next 20% of all occupations	$21 to $25,000/yr.
A	**Average:** within the middle or average 20% of all occupations	$26 to $35,000/yr.
H	**High:** within the next 20% of all occupations	$36 to 45,000/yr.
VH	**Very High:** within the highest 20% of all occupations	over $45,000/yr.

Employment Section

The Job Matching Chart provides four columns of information under its "Employment" heading. Each of these columns provide you with information that you should consider in making a career decision.

Average Earnings: Jobs that require more education, training, or responsibility usually pay better. But some lower-paying jobs could allow you to enjoy your work more. Most occupations have a wide range of earnings. Recent entrants and those in smaller cities often earn much less than the average.

Projected Growth: Our economy is expected to create many new jobs in the years to come. Some jobs will grow more rapidly than others and some will decline. It is helpful to know if the demand for a job is likely to grow. However, you should not select a job just because it is projected to grow quickly. Even where little growth is expected, new jobs are opening as employees retire or go on to other jobs.

Number of Openings: Some occupations employ large numbers of people; others don't. A larger occupation may have many job openings even though it is not growing rapidly. This is often to replace workers who leave. Occupations with many openings may be easier to get, though they sometimes do not pay well.

Unemployment Rate: Those seeking jobs in occupations with low rates of unemployment will often have fewer problems finding a job.

Skills and Working Conditions Sections

The Chart provides primary characteristics of a typical job in that occupation. Columns that are marked indicate that these skills or working conditions are typical. Not all jobs in an occupation are alike, so be careful to understand more about a job before you make important career choices.

Copyright © 1995 • JIST Works, Inc. • Indianapolis, IN 46202 • (317) 264-3720

Job Matching Chart

Column key — SKILLS — Working with Data/Information Skills: 1. Researching and Compiling, 2. Analyzing and Evaluating, 3. Troubleshooting, 4. Artistic Expression — **Working with People Skills:** 5. Instructing, 6. Treating and Advising, 7. Supervising, 8. Persuading, 9. Public Contact — **Working with Things Skills:** 10. Mechanical Ability, 11. Operating a Vehicle — **WORKING CONDITIONS:** 12. Repetitious, 13. Geographically Concentrated, 14. Mobile, 15. Physical Stamina, 16. Part time, 17. Irregular Hours — **EMPLOYMENT:** 18. Average Earnings, 19. Projected Growth, 20. Number of Openings, 21. Unemployment Rate

Occupation	Edu	1	2	3	4	5	6	7	8	9	10	11	12	13	14	15	16	17	18	19	20	21
Management and Financial Occupations																						
General Management Occupations																						
Administrative services managers	HPC		■	■				■											H	L	VL	H
Employment interviewers/personnel specialists	P		■						■	■									VH	H	VH	L
Hotel managers and assistants	C		■	■				■		■								■	VL	VH	H	VH
Inspectors and compliance officers, except construction	C	■	■	■						■					■				H	H	H	L
General managers and top executives	C		■	■				■	■										VH	A	L	H
Government chief executives and legislators	C		■	■				■	■	■					■		■	■	H	VL	A	VL
Personnel, training, and labor relations managers	C		■	■				■		■									VH	VH	H	L
Purchasing agents and managers	PC	■	■	■				■	■										VH	A	H	VL
Financial Occupations																						
Accountants and auditors	C	■	■	■															H	VH	VH	L
Budget analysts	C	■	■	■															A	A	A	H
Cost estimators	C	■	■																A	L	L	H
Financial managers	C	■	■	■				■											VH	H	VH	L
Mathematical, Scientific and Related Occupations																						
Mathematical Occupations																						
Actuaries	C	■	■																A	H	L	L
Computer systems analysts	C	■	■	■															VH	VH	H	L
Computer programmers	C		■	■															H	H	H	L
Mathematicians	C	■	■																H	L	L	A
Operations research analysts	C	■	■	■															VH	VH	H	L
Statistician clerks	C	■	■																A	VL	VL	L
Engineering Occupations																						
Drafters	P		■	■															H	A	H	L
Engineers (aerospace, chemical civil, electrical and electronic industrial, mechanical, metallurgical, mining, nuclear, petroleum)	C	■	■	■															VH	A	H	L
Engineering, science, and data processing managers	C	■	■	■				■											VH	H	H	L
All other engineering technicians and technologists	P	■	■	■							■								H	A	H	A
Scientists and Related Occupations																						
Agricultural scientists	C	■	■																A	A	A	L
Biological Scientists	C	■	■																H	VH	A	L
Foresters	C	■	■											■	■	■			L	L	A	A
Physical scientists (chemists, geologists and geo-physicists meteorologists, physicists, astronomers)	C	■	■																H	A	A	L
Cartographers and geographers	C	■	■																			
Science and mathematics technicians	P	■																	L	H	H	A
Architects and Surveyors																						
Architects	C	■	■		■														VH	H	H	VL
Landscape architects	C	■	■		■										■				H	A	A	L
Surveyors	PC	■	■	■												■			A	A	A	A

Copyright © 1995 • JIST Works, Inc. • Indianapolis, IN 46202 • (317) 264-3720

Job Matching Chart

	EDU	SKILLS — WORKING WITH DATA/INFORMATION SKILLS				SKILLS — WORKING WITH PEOPLE SKILLS					WORKING WITH THINGS SKILLS		WORKING CONDITIONS						EMPLOYMENT			
		1. Researching and Compiling	2. Analyzing and Evaluating	3. Troubleshooting	4. Artistic Expression	5. Instructing	6. Treating and Advising	7. Supervising	8. Persuading	9. Public Contact	10. Mechanical Ability	11. Operating a Vehicle	12. Repetitious	13. Geographically Concentrated	14. Mobile	15. Physical Stamina	16. Part time	17. Irregular Hours	18. Average Earnings	19. Projected Growth	20. Number of Openings	21. Unemployment Rate

Legal, Social Science, and Human Service Occupations

Legal Occupations (also see stenographers and court reporters under administrative support occupations)

Occupation	Edu	1	2	3	4	5	6	7	8	9	10	11	12	13	14	15	16	17	18	19	20	21
Lawyers	C	■	■	■			■		■	■									VH	VH	VH	VL
Paralegals	P	■	■							■									L	H	H	L

Social Scientists and Urban Planners

Occupation	Edu	1	2	3	4	5	6	7	8	9	10	11	12	13	14	15	16	17	18	19	20	21
Anthropologists and archaeologists	C	■	■											■	■				H	A	L	A
Archivists curators and historians	C	■	■																H	A	L	A
Economists	C	■	■																VH	A	A	A
Marketing research analysts	C	■	■						■										H	A	A	H
Psychologists	C	■	■	■			■		■	■									H	A	VH	VL
Urban and regional planners	C	■	■	■					■	■									H	A	A	L
Sociologists	C	■	■						■										H	L	L	H

Social and Recreation Workers

Occupation	Edu	1	2	3	4	5	6	7	8	9	10	11	12	13	14	15	16	17	18	19	20	21
Human services workers	PC	■	■				■			■					■			■	H	VH	VH	L
Recreation workers	HPC					■				■					■	■	■	■	VL	H	H	H
Social workers	C	■	■	■			■		■	■					■				H	VH	VH	L
Clergy	PC					■	■	■	■	■					■			■	A	L	A	VL

Education and Related Occupations

Education Occupations

Occupation	Edu	1	2	3	4	5	6	7	8	9	10	11	12	13	14	15	16	17	18	19	20	21
Adult education teachers	C	■	■	■		■	■										■	■	A	H	H	L
Counselors	C		■	■		■	■		■	■									H	VH	H	VL
Education administrators	C		■	■				■	■	■									VH	H	H	VL
Kindergarten, elementary, and secondary school teachers	C		■	■		■	■										■		H	VH	VH	VL
Preschool workers	HPC			■		■	■		■										L	H	H	L
Teacher aides and education assistants	HP					■											■		VL	VH	VH	A

Library Occupations

Occupation	Edu	1	2	3	4	5	6	7	8	9	10	11	12	13	14	15	16	17	18	19	20	21
Librarians	C	■		■						■							■	■	H	L	A	VL
Library assistants and bookmobile drivers	H									■		■		■			■	■	VL	L	A	A
Library technicians	H	■								■							■	■	L	A	L	H

Health Care Occupations

Occupation	Edu	1	2	3	4	5	6	7	8	9	10	11	12	13	14	15	16	17	18	19	20	21
Health diagnosing practitioners, chiropractors, dentists, optometrists, physicians, podiatrists, veterinarians	C	■	■	■		■	■			■							■	■	VH	H	A	VL
Health services managers	C	■	■	■				■	■										VH	VH	H	L

Health Assessment and Treating Occupations

Occupation	Edu	1	2	3	4	5	6	7	8	9	10	11	12	13	14	15	16	17	18	19	20	21
Dietitians and nutritionists	C		■	■		■	■			■							■		L	A	A	A
Occupational therapists	C		■	■		■	■			■									A	VH	H	L
Pharmacists	C		■	■		■	■			■									H	A	H	VL
Physical therapists	C		■	■		■	■			■						■	■		H	VH	H	VL
Physician assistants	C		■	■		■	■			■								■	H	H	H	L
Recreational therapists	C		■	■		■	■			■				■	■	■			L	H	H	L
Registered nurses	PC		■	■		■	■			■						■	■	■	H	H	VH	VL
Respiratory therapists	PC		■	■		■	■			■									A	VH	H	VL
Speech-language pathologists and audiologists	C		■	■		■	■			■									H	VH	A	VL

Health Technologists and Technicians

Occupation	Edu	1	2	3	4	5	6	7	8	9	10	11	12	13	14	15	16	17	18	19	20	21
Clinical laboratory technologists and technicians	PC		■										■						A	H	H	L

Copyright © 1995 • JIST Works, Inc. • Indianapolis, IN 46202 • (317) 264-3720

Job Matching Chart

Occupation	EDUCATION AND TRAINING	1. Researching and Compiling	2. Analyzing and Evaluating	3. Troubleshooting	4. Artistic Expression	5. Instructing	6. Treating and Advising	7. Supervising	8. Persuading	9. Public Contact	10. Mechanical Ability	11. Operating a Vehicle	12. Repetitious	13. Geographically Concentrated	14. Mobile	15. Physical Stamina	16. Part time	17. Irregular Hours	18. Average Earnings	19. Projected Growth	20. Number of Openings	21. Unemployment Rate
Dental hygienists	P					■	■			■							■		A	VH	H	VL
Opticians, dispensing and measuring	HP									■									A	VH	A	A
EEG Technologists	P	■								■			■						L	VH	H	L
EKG technicians	H	■								■			■						L	VH	H	L
Emergency medical technicians	P		■	■			■			■					■		■	■	L	VH	H	L
Licensed practical nurses	P						■			■						■	■		L	VH	VH	L
Medical record technicians	P	■	■														■		L	VH	V	L
Nuclear medicine, radiologic technicians and technologists	P	■								■									H	VH	VH	VL
Radiological technologists	P	■								■			■						L	VH	H	L
Surgical technicians	P						■			■									L	VH	H	L

Health Service Occupations

Occupation	ED	1	2	3	4	5	6	7	8	9	10	11	12	13	14	15	16	17	18	19	20	21
Dental assistants	H						■			■							■		VL	VH	H	A
Nursing aides, orderlies, and attendants	HP						■			■							■	■	VL	VH	VH	H
Homemaker-home health aides	HP						■			■					■		■		L	VH	VH	L

Communication, Visual Arts, and Performing Arts Occupations

Communications Occupations

Occupation	ED	1	2	3	4	5	6	7	8	9	10	11	12	13	14	15	16	17	18	19	20	21
Broadcast technicians	P			■							■							■	L	L	L	H
Marketing, advertising, and public relations managers	C		■	■	■		■	■	■					■					VH	VH	VH	L
Public relations specialists and publicity writers	C	■	■	■	■				■	■				■					VH	A	A	L
Radio and television announcers and newscasters	HPC	■	■		■					■								■	L	A	A	A
Reporters and correspondents	C	■	■		■				■	■					■			■	L	A	L	A
Writers	PC	■	■		■				■	■									L	H	H	L

Visual Arts Occupations

Occupation	ED	1	2	3	4	5	6	7	8	9	10	11	12	13	14	15	16	17	18	19	20	21
Designers	HPC				■					■									A	A	L	H
Photographers and camera operators	P				■					■	■				■				A	H	H	L
Visual artists	HPC				■														L	A	L	H

Performing Artists

Occupation	ED	1	2	3	4	5	6	7	8	9	10	11	12	13	14	15	16	17	18	19	20	21
Musicians	HC				■					■					■	■	■	■	L	L	A	A
Producers, directors, actors, and entertainers	PC	■	■	■	■	■		■	■	■					■			■	—	VH	H	VH

Sales and Related Occupations

Marketing, Retail and Sales Occupations

Occupation	ED	1	2	3	4	5	6	7	8	9	10	11	12	13	14	15	16	17	18	19	20	21
Cashiers	H									■			■				■	■	VL	H	VH	VH
Counter and rental clerks	H									■			■				■	■	VL	VH	H	H
Manufacturers' and wholesale sales representatives	C	■	■	■		■			■	■					■				L	L	L	H
Retail salesworkers	H								■	■							■	■	VL	H	VH	H
Securities and financial services sales workers	C	■	■				■		■	■									VH	VH	H	L
Services sales representatives	H					■			■	■									L	H	H	L
Travel agents	H	■		■					■	■							■	■	VL	VH	H	L
Wholesale and retail buyers	PC	■	■	■				■		■									H	A	H	L

Insurance Occupations (also see adjusters, investigators, and collectors under administrative support occupations; and actuaries under mathematical occupations)

Occupation	ED	1	2	3	4	5	6	7	8	9	10	11	12	13	14	15	16	17	18	19	20	21
Insurance sales workers	PC	■	■				■		■	■									H	A	H	VL
Underwriters	PC	■	■																A	H	A	VL

Copyright © 1995 • JIST Works, Inc. • Indianapolis, IN 46202 • (317) 264-3720

Job Matching Chart

Occupation	EDUCATION AND TRAINING	1. Researching and Compiling	2. Analyzing and Evaluating	3. Troubleshooting	4. Artistic Expression	5. Instructing	6. Treating and Advising	7. Supervising	8. Persuading	9. Public Contact	10. Mechanical Ability	11. Operating a Vehicle	12. Repetitious	13. Geographically Concentrated	14. Mobile	15. Physical Stamina	16. Part-time	17. Irregular Hours	18. Average Earnings	19. Projected Growth	20. Number of Openings	21. Unemployment Rate
Real Estate Occupations																						
Property and real estate managers	C	■	■	■				■	■	■					■				A	VH	H	L
Real estate agents, brokers, and appraisers	HP	■	■	■			■		■	■					■		■	■	H	A	H	VL
Administrative Support Occupations																						
Adjusters, investigators, and collectors	HPC	■	■							■									L	A	H	L
Bank tellers	HP									■				■			■		VL	VL	VL	A
Clerical supervisors and managers	HPC		■	■				■											H	A	VH	VL
Computer operators	P			■														■	A	A	H	A
Credit clerks and authorizers	H	■												■					A	H	VH	A
Dispatchers	H			■						■				■				■	A	H	H	A
General office clerks	H																■		L	H	VH	A
Postal mail carriers	H									■		■		■	■	■		■	H	H	H	VL
Mail clerks	H													■					L	L	A	H
Material, recording, scheduling, and distributing occupations (stock clerks, shipping and receiving clerks)	H													■					L	A	H	H
Messengers	H									■		■	■	■	■	■	■		L	L	A	H
Postal service clerks	H									■				■			■		H	L	L	A
Receptionists and other information clerks	H									■				■					VL	VH	VH	H
Records clerks (billing, bookkeeping, accounting, brokerage, file, order, payroll, and personnel clerks)	H	■												■					VL	L	H	L
Secretaries	H			■						■									L	A	VH	A
Stenographers	P													■			■		L	VL	VL	VL
Telephone operators	H									■				■				■	L	VL	VL	H
Typists and word processors	H													■					L	VL	VL	VL
Service Occupations																						
Protective Service Occupations																						
Correction officers	H							■										■	A	VH	H	VL
Firefighters	H		■					■	■		■				■	■		■	A	H	H	L
Guards	H									■				■			■	■	VL	VH	VH	H
Police detectives and patrol officers	H	■	■	■				■						■	■				A	H	VH	VL
Food and Beverage Preparation and Service Occupations																						
Chefs	P					■		■										■	A	VH	VH	L
Cooks and other kitchen workers	H												■				■	■	VL	VH	VH	L
Food and beverage service occupations	H									■			■				■	■	VL	VH	VH	L
Restaurant and food service managers	C		■	■				■		■								■	L	VH	H	L
Personal Service and Facility Maintenance Occupations																						
Animal caretakers, except farm	H														■	■		■	L	VH	H	A
Barbers	P									■				■			■	■	L	VL	VL	VL
Gardeners and groundskeepers (except farm)	—										■	■	■	■	■	■		■	VL	VH	VH	VH
Janitors and cleaners	—												■		■	■	■	■	VL	A	VH	VH
Private household workers	—													■	■	■	■	■	VL	VL	VL	H
Agricultural, Forestry, Fishing, and Related Occupations																						
Farm operators and managers	PC		■	■				■				■		■	■	■		■	L	A	A	A

Copyright © 1995 • JIST Works, Inc. • Indianapolis, IN 46202 • (317) 264-3720

Job Matching Chart

Occupation	Education and Training	1. Researching and Compiling	2. Analyzing and Evaluating	3. Troubleshooting	4. Artistic Expression	5. Instructing	6. Treating and Advising	7. Supervising	8. Persuading	9. Public Contact	10. Mechanical Ability	11. Operating a Vehicle	12. Repetitious	13. Geographically Concentrated	14. Mobile	15. Physical Stamina	16. Part time	17. Irregular Hours	18. Average Earnings	19. Projected Growth	20. Number of Openings	21. Unemployment Rate
Fishers, hunters, and trappers	—													■	■	■	■	■	A	L	L	VH
Timber cutting and logging workers	—													■	■	■		■	VL	VL	VL	VH

Mechanics, Installers and Repairers (also see aircraft mechanics under air transportation occupations)

Occupation	Education and Training	1	2	3	4	5	6	7	8	9	10	11	12	13	14	15	16	17	18	19	20	21
Automotive body repairers	P			■							■					■			A	H	H	A
Electronic equipment repairers (commercial and industrial electronic equipment, communications equipment, home entertainment, and telephone repairers)	P			■						■	■				■	■			A	VL	L	L
Home appliance and power tool repairers	HP			■						■	■				■	■			A	L	VL	L
Mechanics (automotive diesel, farm equipment, mobile heavy equipment, motorcycle, boat, small engine, and general maintenance mechanics)	P			■						■	■					■			L	A	H	L
Musical instrument repairers and tuners	—			■						■	■				■	■			L	L	A	H
Vending machine servicers and repairers	H			■						■	■				■	■			VL	L	A	A

Construction and Related Occupations

Occupation	Education and Training	1	2	3	4	5	6	7	8	9	10	11	12	13	14	15	16	17	18	19	20	21
Bricklayers and stonemasons	HP										■				■	■			A	A	H	VH
Carpenters	HP														■	■			A	A	VH	VH
Carpet installers	HP													■	■	■			L	A	A	H
Concrete masons and terazzo workers	HP														■	■			A	A	A	VH
Construction and building inspectors	HP		■	■					■						■	■			A	A	A	L
Construction contractors and managers	PC	■	■	■			■	■	■						■				H	L	VH	L
Drywall workers and lathers	HP														■	■			A	H	H	VH
Electricians	HP			■							■				■	■			H	H	VH	H
Elevator installers and repairers	H			■							■				■	■			A	A	A	L
Glaziers	HP														■	■			A	H	A	H
Heating, air-conditioning, and refrigeration technicians	HP			■							■				■	■			A	A	H	A
Insulation workers	HP												■		■	■			L	H	A	VH
Line installers and cable splicers	—			■							■				■	■			H	VL	VL	L
Painters and paperhangers	HP												■		■	■	■		L	H	VH	L
Plasterers	HP												■		■	■			H	A	L	H
Plumbers, pipefitters, and steamfitters	P			■							■				■	■			H	A	H	H
Roofers	HP												■		■	■			L	H	H	H
Roustabouts	—										■			■	■	■		■	L	VL	VL	VH
Sheet-metal workers	P														■	■			L	A	H	H
Structural and reinforcing ironworkers	HP										■			■	■	■			H	A	A	VH
Hand tilesetters	HP												■		■	■			A	H	L	VH

Production Occupations

Plant and Systems Operators

Occupation	Education and Training	1	2	3	4	5	6	7	8	9	10	11	12	13	14	15	16	17	18	19	20	21
Electric power generating plant operators and power dispatchers	H		■	■							■							■	A	L	L	H
Stationary engineers	H			■							■							■	A	L	L	VL
Water and wastewater treatment plant operators	H	■	■	■							■							■	A	H	A	VL

Printing Occupations

Occupation	Education and Training	1	2	3	4	5	6	7	8	9	10	11	12	13	14	15	16	17	18	19	20	21
Prepress workers	H			■							■							■	A	VL	VL	H
Printing press operators	H			■							■		■					■	A	A	H	A
Bindery workers	H			■							■		■						VL	A	L	A

Copyright © 1995 • JIST Works, Inc. • Indianapolis, IN 46202 • (317) 264-3720

Job Matching Chart

	EDUCATION AND TRAINING	1. Researching and Compiling	2. Analyzing and Evaluating	3. Troubleshooting	4. Artistic Expression	5. Instructing	6. Treating and Advising	7. Supervising	8. Persuading	9. Public Contact	10. Mechanical Ability	11. Operating a Vehicle	12. Repetitious	13. Geographically Concentrated	14. Mobile	15. Physical Stamina	16. Part time	17. Irregular Hours	18. Average Earnings	19. Projected Growth	20. Number of Openings	21. Unemployment Rate
Textile, Apparel, and Furnishing Occupations																						
Apparel workers	—												■						VL	L	H	L
Shoe and leather workers and repairers	—							■					■					■	VL	L	L	H
Textile machinery operators	H			■							■		■	■				■	L	L	A	A
Upholsterers	H																		L	L	L	A
Miscellaneous Production Occupations																						
Blue-collar worker supervisors	H			■				■										■	H	L	VH	L
Boilermakers	H	■	■								■				■	■			A	VL	VL	H
Butcher, meat, and poultry cutters	H							■					■						L	VL	VL	H
Handlers, equipment cleaners, helpers, and laborers	—												■			■			VL	A	H	L
Industrial machinery repairers	P	■	■								■				■	■		■	H	L	H	A
Millwrights	P	■	■								■				■	■		■	H	A	A	H
Industrial production managers	C	■	■					■											VH	VL	A	L
Inspectors, testers, and graders	H	■	■										■					■	L	VL	L	H
Jewelers	P			■						■	■								L	A	H	A
Machinists	P			■							■							■	A	L	H	A
Tool and die makers	P			■							■							■	H	L	L	L
Metal and plastics working machine operators	H			■							■		■					■	L	VL	VL	VH
Numerical control machine tool operators	H			■							■		■					■	H	A	L	L
Painting and coating machine operators	—												■						L	L	VL	VH
Photographic process workers	H												■				■	■	VL	A	L	A
Precision assemblers	H			■							■		■						VL	L	L	A
Tool programmers, numerical control	PC	■	■								■								H	H	L	L
Welders, cutters, and welding machine operators	P										■		■			■		■	A	L	A	VH
Woodworking occupations	H										■		■						L	A	A	VH
Transportation Occupations																						
Air Transportation Occupations																						
Aircraft pilots	C			■								■			■			■	VH	H	A	H
Air traffic controllers	HPC	■	■															■	H	L	L	L
Aircraft mechanics and engine specialists	P			■				■								■		■	VH	H	L	L
Flight attendants	HP			■				■							■			■	VL	L	H	H
Ground Transportation Occupations																						
Busdrivers	H			■						■	■	■		■			■		A	VH	VH	A
Material moving equipment operators	HP										■	■							A	L	A	VH
Rail transportation occupations	H			■							■		■					■	A	VL	VL	A
Truck drivers	H			■							■	■		■	■			■	A	H	VH	H
Water Transportation Occupations																						
Marine engineers and captains	C			■		■					■	■		■				■	H	L	VL	VH
Mates and seamen	H			■							■			■	■			■	L	L	VL	VH

Copyright © 1995 • JIST Works, Inc. • Indianapolis, IN 46202 • (317) 264-3720

My Top Jobs Worksheet

Directions: *Review the Job Matching Chart carefully. Select the three to five occupations that most interest you for long-term career possibilities. Do not exclude those that require more training or education for now. For each one, complete the worksheet section that follows.*

Job #1: _____

Why did you select this job? _____

_____

_____

What more do you need to find out about this job? _____

_____

_____

Job #2: _____

Why did you select this job? _____

_____

_____

What more do you need to find out about this job? _____

_____

_____

Job #3: _____

Why did you select this job? _____

_____

_____

What more do you need to find out about this job? _____

_____

_____

Job #4: _____

Why did you select this job? _____

_____

_____

What more do you need to find out about this job? _____

_____

_____

Copyright © 1995 • JIST Works, Inc. • Indianapolis, IN 46202 • (317) 264-3720

Job #5: _____

Why did you select this job? _____

_____

_____

What more do you need to find out about this job? _____

_____

_____

Where to Get More Information

Before making an important career decision, you should get more information on each of the jobs that interest you. Some of the best sources of career information are listed below.

Occupational Outlook Handbook **(O.O.H):** Published every two years by the U.S. Department of Labor, this book is available in most libraries and schools. All the jobs listed in the Job Matching Chart are described in the O.O.H. One-, or two-page descriptions give information on working conditions, pay rates, training or education needed, projection for growth, and many other details. If you want to learn more about any of the jobs listed on the Chart, this is the best place to start.

America's Top 300 Jobs: This is a version of the O.O.H. that is sold in bookstores and also may be available in many libraries.

The Complete Guide for Occupational Exploration **(C.G.O.E.):** This book lists more than 12,000 jobs within 12 major interest areas and increasingly specific subgroups. The arrangement makes it easy to locate jobs that interest you. Each grouping includes information about the jobs in that group, skills and interests needed, as well as typical education and other details. The jobs are also cross-referenced in useful ways such as industry, types of skills required, or jobs related to those on the Job Matching Chart.

The Enhanced Guide for Occupational Exploration **(E.G.O.E.):** Organized like the C.G.O.E. and includes brief descriptions for 2,500 jobs.

Dictionary of Occupational Titles **(D.O.T.):** Published by the Department of Labor, it provides brief descriptions of the more than 12,000 jobs listed in the C.G.O.E. It is hard to use but provides lots of information.

The Library: Most libraries have books, videos, computer look up programs and other resource materials on a variety of careers. Ask the librarian for help in finding information about the jobs that interest you.

Schools and Programs: Most schools and career training programs have information on careers and on the educational programs that prepare for them. Some provide testing, counseling, computerized information systems, and other services to help you make a good decision. Find out about and use these services if they are available to you.

People: Ask friends, relatives, and others to tell you what they know about the jobs that interest you. They also may know about other jobs you might consider. Once you get interested in a type of job, find workers who have this kind of job. Ask them what they do or don't like about it, how they got started, and what advice they can give you about getting a job in that area.

Work in the Field: Once you are sure about a career interest, a good way to learn more about it is to get a job in that area. Often, you can find entry-level jobs that don't require special training. You would then be in a good position to decide to stay there, get additional training, or try something else.

Don't Just Look for "Any" Job

The rest of this book will teach you how to find and succeed on a job. But before you continue your education or begin your job search, it is important to know what sort of job you want. Even if you aren't sure, you should at least decide what sort of job interests you more than others. For example, if you enjoy working with people, consider looking for a job that gives you lots of contact with other people — such as customers. If you like to listen to music, perhaps you could look for a job in a music store.

Even entry-level and part-time jobs can help you learn more about a career area that interests you. So don't take just any job, think about what you really want to do — and then look for a job that comes as close as possible. Why not?

Copyright © 1995 • JIST Works, Inc. • Indianapolis, IN 46202 • (317) 264-3720

5

Traditional Job-Hunting Techniques

Some Work Better Than Others

Looking for a job is hard work. If you are lucky, you may find one quickly. But finding even an entry-level, minimum wage job can take a long time if you don't know how to look. The average adult spends three to five months finding a new job. When unemployment rates are high, you can be out of work even longer. But some people find jobs faster than others, even in times of high unemployment. What do they do differently?

Finding a job takes more than luck. Some job search methods work better than others. The best methods can help you find better jobs and can even reduce the time it takes to find them. Most of the rest of this book will teach you how to use these methods.

Copyright © 1995 • JIST Works, Inc. • Indianapolis, IN 46202 • (317) 264-3720

What Do You Think?

Directions: *People use many different methods to find jobs. In the following spaces, list as many methods as you can.*

_____   _____

_____   _____

_____   _____

_____   _____

Some of these techniques are used by more people than others. And some methods work better than others. Think about your own experiences and those of people you know. What five job search techniques do you think most people use to get their jobs? List them here, beginning with the most often used, followed by the second, and so on.

1. _____

2. _____

3. _____

4. _____

5. _____

Brief Review of Traditional Methods

Did you list the traditional methods most job seekers use?

Traditional Methods:

- Answering want ads
- Using the government's employment service *(sometimes called the Unemployment Office)*
- Using a private employment agency
- Sending out resumes
- Filling out applications

Copyright © 1995 • JIST Works, Inc. • Indianapolis, IN 46202 • (317) 264-3720

All these methods work for some people. In fact, these techniques are used by most job seekers and many of them do get jobs. But these are not the best methods. If you cross off these methods from your top five, what is left? If your list includes personal contacts or something like it, you are on target. Making personal contacts is one of the most effective methods you can use. Another effective method is making direct contact with an employer — usually after someone has told you that a job may be open.

How People Find Jobs — Facts and Figures

You already know which two job-search methods are most effective, but can you guess how effective? A number of the most often used job search techniques are listed here, beginning with the most frequently used methods. Look over the list, then guess what percentage of job seekers used each method to get their jobs. Write the percentage in the first column of the following chart.

What Percentage of Job Seekers Used These Methods to Find Their Jobs?

Method	Your Guess	Actual
Heard about opening from someone:	_____	_____
Contacted employer directly:	_____	_____
Answered want ad:	_____	_____
Referred by private employment agency:	_____	_____
Referred by state employment service:	_____	_____
Took civil service government tests:	_____	_____
Other Methods:	_____	_____

You can find the correct answers at the end of this chapter. Look them up and enter the correct percentages in the second column.

Copyright © 1995 • JIST Works, Inc. • Indianapolis, IN 46202 • (317) 264-3720

A Review of Traditional Job-Seeking Methods

Most people use more than one technique to find job openings. For example, one person might read want ads, fill out applications, and ask friends for job leads. Each of these methods works for some people. Other methods are used by other job seekers. Which methods are best for you? This and the next several chapters will help you find out.

Most people use one or more of the traditional job search methods. While they are not always the most effective methods, many people do find jobs through them. Here are some comments on using them effectively.

Reading the Want Ads

About 15 percent of jobs are found through the want ads. That means about one in every seven job seekers finds his or her job this way. While this is not a large number, want ads are worth looking at on a regular basis.

Some Tips for Using the Want Ads

Read the want ads on a regular basis. The Sunday and Wednesday editions of the newspaper usually have the most ads. Look at each and every ad. The ones you are interested in may not be listed in an obvious way. For example, a secretarial job could be listed under "Secretary" or "General Office" or "Clerical" or other headings.

Respond to any ad that sounds interesting, even if you don't have all the qualifications listed. Employers sometimes list things they do not require to limit the response. If possible, try to contact the advertiser directly. Instead of sending in a resume or completing an application, call and ask for the person who supervises the position you want. Ask for an appointment to discuss the position. It sometimes works and can reduce your chances of being screened out.

Also, look at old want ads. The same organizations may have openings now that have not yet been advertised. As much as possible, read want ads during the evenings and weekends. Save weekdays for making direct contacts with employers.

The Employment Service

The government has set up a system of offices to help people find jobs and to handle unemployment claims. These offices are given different names in different states. For example, it might be called the "Department of Labor" or "Employment Security." Many people call it the "Unemployment Office" since it is where you go to file for unemployment benefits.

Copyright © 1995 • JIST Works, Inc. • Indianapolis, IN 46202 • (317) 264-3720

All of these agencies list job openings given to them by local employers. You can go there and ask for referrals to jobs that you are qualified for, and they will send you to those employers that have listed openings.

These government agencies never charge a fee. Some also provide free testing to help you know what jobs you can consider. A few provide training in how to get a job or other special services.

Tips for Using the Employment Service

Only about 6 percent of all job seekers get their jobs through the Employment Service. And some studies have found that only 5 percent of all available jobs are listed here.

While that may not sound like much, I suggest that you visit the Employment Service office each week during your job search. Try to see the same counselor or staff person each time so he or she can get to know you. The staff often see hundreds of people each week but will refer you to the better job openings if you impress them.

Ask if your local office provides other services. If so, consider using one or more of them since they are often free. In some areas of the country, this office may list as many as 30 percent of the jobs in your area. This is another reason to use this free service.

Private Employment Agencies

Private employment agencies are businesses that charge a fee for any job that you accept through them. These people will often ask you to sign an agreement that will require you to pay them 15 percent or more of a year's wages for any job they refer you to that results in a job offer.

Tips for Using Private Employment Agencies

Unless the employer pays the fee, using a private employment agency is not a good idea for most people. Only about 5 percent of all workers get their jobs in this way. Many of these agency workers find their clients' jobs though calling up employers and asking if they have any job openings. This is something you can do yourself.

Some agencies will also pressure you to accept any job that they can talk you into so they can collect their fee. Watch out for want ads placed by these agencies, too. The advertised job may not exist, and they may refer you to another one paying less money.

Only one out of 20 people using an agency gets a job from them. While this is a 95 percent failure rate, some people can benefit from them. Some research indicates that more people benefit from using a private employment agency than in the past. If your skills are in demand and you have a clear job objective, an

Copyright © 1995 • JIST Works, Inc. • Indianapolis, IN 46202 • (317) 264-3720

agency is more likely to help you. Ask to be referred to jobs where the employer pays the fee. And do not feel pressured to accept a job you do not want.

Do not sign any agreement until you take it home and read it carefully. If you are pressured to sign anything during your first visit, refuse to sign it and leave.

If you do decide to use a private employment agency, make sure that you continue to look for jobs on your own. Any agreement you sign should not require you to pay a fee for a job that you find yourself or limit your job search in any way.

Mailing Resumes

You could get lucky, but resumes sent to no one in particular will probably end up in the trash. Expect a 5 percent or lower response rate and even fewer interviews.

Tips for Using the Resume

Another chapter in this book will cover how to write and use a resume. But you should know that very few people get a job through sending out resumes to people they do not know. It is almost always better to contact the employer in person. Then send your resume before the interview.

Filling Out Applications

Many people go to employers and ask to complete an application for employment. These forms are reviewed in more detail later in this book. In most cases, applications are not a good way to be considered for a job.

Tips for Using Applications

Applications are often used to screen people out. They are most effective for entry-level jobs such as those often held by young people. Your best approach is to ask to talk to the person who will make the hiring decision. Even if you are required to fill out an application first, you should still ask for an interview. Many small businesses do not even have applications. It is always better to ask to see the person in charge directly. Fill out an application if you are asked to, but don't expect it to get you an interview.

Other Job Search Methods

The next chapter reviews the two most effective methods for getting job leads. They are getting leads from people you already know and making direct contacts with employers. These methods will be reviewed in detail there. Following are some other ideas.

Copyright © 1995 • JIST Works, Inc. • Indianapolis, IN 46202 • (317) 264-3720

Volunteering

If you lack experience or are not getting job offers, consider volunteering to work for free. Perhaps you could offer your services for a day or even a week to show an employer what you can do. Promise that if things don't work out, you will leave with no hard feelings. This really does work, and many employers will give you a chance because they like your attitude.

School Placement Office

If you are lucky enough to have a school counselor or placement staff, get to know them soon. If they have job listings, follow their advice and go to any interviews they set up. Never miss an interview they send you to.

Professional Associations

Many professions have special publications for people who work in that field. They are often a good source of information and some list job openings. Local branches of national organizations sometimes list job openings, too. They are worth checking into.

Civil Service Jobs

Jobs with various government agencies are a major part of our labor market. Applying for them often requires special tests and other procedures. Find out about local, state, and federal jobs by contacting the personnel divisions for each. They are listed in your phone book. It is worth a visit to find out more about how they hire people. But it often takes a long time to get an interview for one of these jobs. And even longer before you get an offer. Even so, they may be worth looking into.

Self-Employment

If you want to join the growing number of people who work for themselves, start at the library. There are many helpful books and other resource materials there. Ask the librarian for help! Another good idea is to work in a business like the one you want to start yourself. There is no better way to learn how to run a similar business.

Start at the Bottom

If you are being told you do not have enough experience, take an entry-level job in the field you want. Look for ways to work your way up as quickly as possible. Learn as much as you can, let the boss know you want to move up, and take on difficult tasks.

Consider Additional Training or Education

Many of the better jobs require special training or advanced education. If a job interests you, it is often worth getting the education it requires. Additional training and education often quickly pays off in additional earnings and advancement opportunities. For example, the average wages of a college graudate are about $15,000 above those of a high school graduate. Many of the fastest-growing jobs require education or training beyond the high school level. These jobs often pay better and have more potential for the future than jobs that do not require special training. While a college degree is required for more and more jobs, many good paying jobs require training or education that lasts from six months to two years. Look into financial aid that is available through many schools. Even if you can't afford to go to school full time, you can often go to night classes or work an evening job that allows you to take classes during the day. Once you are sure about what you want to do long term, find a way to get the education or training it requires. Few people regret doing this, so don't let this be a barrier to your doing what you really want.

Answers to How People Find Jobs

Over the years, there have been various studies done to find out how people actually find their jobs. There are a number of ways to approach this topic and many of the studies don't come up with the same data. One of the biggest surveys of unemployed people is routinely done as part of the Current Population Survey (CPS) — a survey of thousands of households in the U.S. that is done on a regular basis. While this survey asks about their status as employed or unemployed — and what job search methods they are using to find a job — it does not ask what job search methods actually worked.

Back in the 1970s, there was a CPS study that did ask which techniques actually worked but that information may not be valid now. Since then, there have been a variety of studies on how people find jobs but none were with as large a group. So, having looked at the available research on how people actually find jobs, I present the following data on the major techniques. These figures should be considered approximate but they are supported by a variety of research findings.

How People Find Jobs	
Heard about opening from someone	35%
Contacted employer directly	30
Answered want ad	14
Referred by private employment agency	6
Referred by state employment service	5
Took civil service (government) tests	2
Other methods (referred by school, union referral, placed ads in journals, etc.)	8

60

Copyright © 1995 • JIST Works, Inc. • Indianapolis, IN 46202 • (317) 264-3720

6

The Two Best Job Search Methods

About 70% of All Jobs Are Found Using These Two Methods

wo job search methods are more effective than all others put together. This chapter shows you what they are and how to use them. But before I present them in detail, there are some other things you need to know about how to find job leads.

The Hidden Job Market

Most jobs are not advertised. As you saw in chapter 5, fewer than 15 percent of all people get their jobs through the want ads. The few jobs that are advertised there are soon known to anyone who is looking for a job. Jobs available through private and government employment agencies also are considered public knowledge. Anyone can find out about them.

But these advertised openings add up to only about 25 percent of all job openings. Most of the rest are hidden from you if you use traditional job search methods!

*Look at the following chart. It shows that only two job seeking methods —
direct contact with employers and getting leads from people you know — are
used to find most jobs.*

Using both of these methods, you can find out about unadvertised job openings, where about 75 percent of all jobs are found. For these reasons, most of this chapter emphasizes *nontraditional* or *informal* job seeking methods.

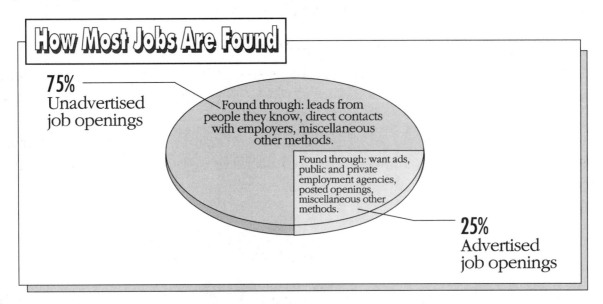

How Most Jobs Are Found

75%
Unadvertised
job openings

Found through: leads from
people they know, direct contacts
with employers, miscellaneous
other methods.

Found through: want ads,
public and private
employment agencies,
posted openings,
miscellaneous other
methods.

25%
Advertised
job openings

Why Most Jobs Are Not Advertised

*Most jobs are never advertised. Why not? Think about this for a bit. Then
write three reasons in the following spaces:*

Why Are Most Jobs Not Advertised?

1. _____

2. _____

3. _____

**Employers don't advertise job openings for many
reasons. The most common reasons are:**

- They don't like to.
- They often don't need to.

Copyright © 1995 • JIST Works, Inc. • Indianapolis, IN 46202 • (317) 264-3720

Let's look at each reason.

Employers Don't Like to Advertise

When employers put an ad in the paper, they have to interview all sorts of strangers. Most employers are not trained interviewers and don't enjoy it. They have to interview people who do their best to create a good impression. And they have to eliminate most of them by finding their weaknesses. It's not fun for either side.

Often, Employers Don't Need to Advertise

Most jobs are filled before advertising is needed. The employer may already know someone who seems to be right for the job. Or someone hears about the job and gets an interview before it is advertised.

Often, employers hire someone who's been recommended to them by a friend or associate. Employers are much more comfortable hiring a person they know is good rather than someone they don't know at all.

The Four Stages of a Job Opening

If you were depending just on the want ads, you would never know about the good jobs that are not advertised. Someone else would get them. But how do you find these openings if they're not advertised? Here is the answer. You have to learn to find employers before they advertise the job you want.

Most jobs don't simply pop open. They are created over a period of time. Carefully study the illustration that follows. It shows you how most jobs open up and get filled. Notice that about 75 percent of all jobs get filled in the first, second, or third stage of a job opening. That is why so few are ever advertised — most jobs are filled before they need to be advertised.

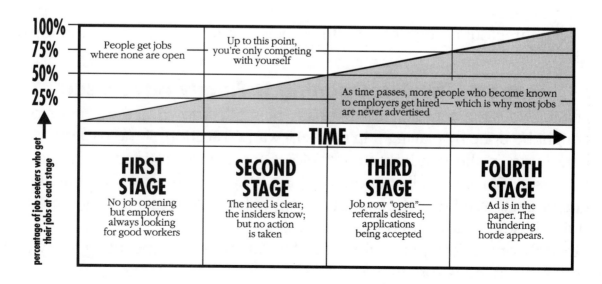

More Details on the Four Stages of a Job Opening

Let's look at the four stages of a job openign in more detail.

Stage 1: There Is No Job Opening Now

If you were to contact an employer at this stage and ask if they had any openings, they would say "no." If you were going about your job search in the traditional way, you would not talk to this employer. Yet, should an opening come up at any time in the future, this employer would first consider people already known.

About 25 percent of all people get their jobs by being known by employers during this stage.

Stage 2: No Formal Job Opening Exists, But One or More Insiders Know

As time goes on, someone inside an organization knows that there is a need for someone in the future. It may be that business is picking up. Or a new product or marketing plan is in the works. Or maybe someone is getting ready to leave or be fired. Sometimes even the boss won't know. If you ask if there is a job opening at this stage, you would probably be told "no" once again. And most job seekers would keep on looking somewhere else, not seeing the job right before them.

About half of all jobs are filled by people who come to know an employer before the end of this stage.

Stage 3: A Formal Opening Now Exists, But It Has Not Yet Been Advertised

At some point in time, the boss will finally say that, yes, there is a job opening. People who work there know about it but it is often days or even weeks before it is advertised. If you just happen to ask if there is a job opening, you will finally be told that there is.

About three out of four jobs are filled before it leaves this stage and needs to be advertised.

Stage 4: The Job Opening Is Finally Advertised

If a job does not get filled, it will finally be made known to the general public. This might be done by placing it in the help wanted section of the paper. Or a sign may be hung in the window, the employment service notified, or some other method used. Since virtually anyone looking for a job can now find out about it, dozens or even hundreds of people now apply for it. And that is why the competition for these few advertised jobs is so fierce.

But only one in four jobs make it this far. All the others, including many of the best ones, are filled before they need to be advertised.

Copyright © 1995 • JIST Works, Inc. • Indianapolis, IN 46202 • (317) 264-3720

What Do the Four Stages of a Job Opening Mean to You?

To succeed in your job search, you have to get to employers before they advertise their jobs. You need to redefine how to get a job. This means getting in to talk to employers in the first, second, or third stages of a job opening.

Of course, you should also go after advertised openings. But you must realize that most jobs will not be advertised at all. To find those jobs, you have to use nontraditional job search methods. Most of the rest of this book will teach you nontraditional job seeking methods. These methods have been proven to work better than more traditional approaches. They can help you find better jobs and they can help you find them in less time.

Small Organizations—Where the Jobs Are

While many people use job search techniques that make sense for larger organizations, most of us now work for smaller organizations. Smaller companies usually don't even have a personnel office or advertise their jobs, so techniques such as sending resumes, completing applications, and reading want ads just don't work well with them.

As the chart that follows shows, more than 70 percent of all nongovernmental workers now work in small organizations. More importantly, most of the new jobs in our economy now come from small organizations. More than 50 percent of us work in organizations with fewer than 100 employees. The opportunities in these small organizations often are better than in large companies. Smaller companies often are more willing to hire younger workers and many more experienced workers also have found opportunities there. Look at the following chart to see the importance of small organizations in your job search.

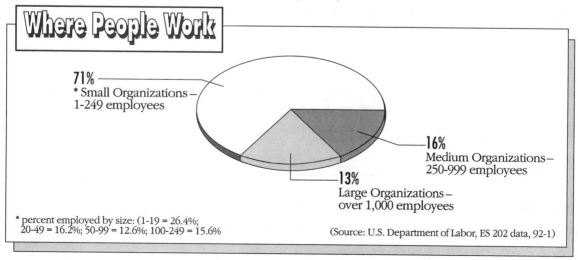

Where People Work

71%
* Small Organizations—
1-249 employees

16%
Medium Organizations—
250-999 employees

13%
Large Organizations—
over 1,000 employees

* percent employed by size: (1-19 = 26.4%;
20-49 = 16.2%; 50-99 = 12.6%; 100-249 = 15.6%

(Source: U.S. Department of Labor, ES 202 data, 92-1)

Many of the nontraditional methods presented in this book are most effective with smaller employers. This is the way our economy is headed. But the methods also work well with larger, more formal organizations, too.

The Most Effective Nontraditional Job Search Methods

You have already learned that traditional job search methods are not very effective. The rest of this chapter reviews two job search methods that get better results for most people — *warm contacts* and *cold contacts*.

When you ask for help or advice from people you know, you are using warm contacts. When you contact people you don't know, you are talking to cold contacts.

Both methods can be very effective if used properly. Since it is often easier to contact people you know, we will begin with warm contacts.

Warm Contacts — Getting Jobs Leads from People in Your Network

A network is an informal group of people who have something in common. As a job seeker, your network is made up of all the people who can help you — and the people they know. Networking is the process you use in contacting these people. You may be surprised at how many people you can meet this way. Let's look at how this works.

Start with the People You Know

Your friends and relatives are the people who are most willing to help you find a job. And they can provide valuable leads to the people they know. To see how networking can work for you, begin by writing the names of three friends or relatives on the following lines.

1. _____
2. _____
3. _____

Now let's take the first person on the list as an example. If you asked that person for the names of two people, you would have two new contacts. Your network would look like the following:

Copyright © 1995 • JIST Works, Inc. • Indianapolis, IN 46202 • (317) 264-3720

One Person in Your Network Leads to Two Others

Referral 1   **Referral 2**

Someone You Know

If you asked each of these referrals for two names and then continued the process, your network would soon look like this:

Your Network Expands

Incredible Arithmetic

The numbers of people you could contact this way are amazing. For example, if you kept getting two referrals from each person, you would have 1,024 people in your network after only the tenth level of contacts. And that is starting with only one person!

Networking is a simple idea and it does work. It helps you meet potential employers you would not find using any other method. These potential employers are a friend of a friend of a friend. And they will be willing to see you for this reason.

More Tips on Developing Your Network of Contacts

Because networking is such an effective way to get job leads, I am presenting additional ways to make your network truly effective.

Have Clear Objectives

You need to have clear objectives before you go out to see someone in your network. Write what you think your objectives should be:

Experience shows that you need to meet the following objectives in each of your networking contacts.

1. Select Good Contacts

You can begin networking with anyone who knows people and is willing to talk to you. The people you are then referred to are likely to know even more about the job you want. Each referral will try to be helpful and refer you to someone who knows even more than he or she does.

2. Present Yourself Well

You need to convince the people you see that you have the skills to do a good job. They must like you too, or it will be very difficult to get them to help you. Tell them what sort of job you are looking for and what skills, experience, and other credentials you have for that job.

3. Get Two Referrals

Sometimes the person you talk to knows of an opening for someone like you. But more often, this person does not. Your objective is to get the names of two people who could also help you in your job search.

Copyright © 1995 • JIST Works, Inc. • Indianapolis, IN 46202 • (317) 264-3720

The Three Questions to Ask to Get Referrals

For you to expand your network of contacts, it is important that you get names of other people to contact from each person in your network. To do so, you need to ask the three questions I listed below. Ask each one until you get the name of two people you can contact.

REMEMBER

The Three Essential Questions to Get Referrals

1. Do you know of anyone who might have a job opening in my field? *(If no, then ask...)*

2. Do you know of anyone who might know of someone who would? *(If still no, then ask...)*

3. Do you know someone who knows lots of people?

Most people don't ask the second or third question. And, because they don't, they do not get the good referrals that many people would be willing to give them if they had only asked. Try them, the questions do work!

Plugging into Networking Groups

You already know many groups of people who can help you. The following chart shows a list of groups that other job seeekers have used. You probably can think of additional groups who can be part of your network.

Sample Networking Groups

Friends	Neighbors	Relatives
Friends of parents	My friends' parents	Former employers
Former coworkers	Classmates	Former classmates
Members of my church or religous group	Members of social clubs	Members of sports groups
People who sell me things (at the store, insurance, etc.)	People who provide me with services (hair stylist, counselor, mechanic, etc.)	Members of a professional organization I belong to (or could quickly join)

Copyright © 1995 • JIST Works, Inc. • Indianapolis, IN 46202 • (317) 264-3720

Networking Worksheet — Groups of People I Know

Directions: Write your own list of at least ten groups on the following form. Since everyone has friends and most have relatives, they have already been listed on the form. Use our examples for ideas and add others to your list that make sense to you.

Friends
Relatives
_____   _____
_____   _____
_____   _____
_____   _____
_____   _____
_____   _____
_____   _____
_____   _____

Each of the groups you have listed can be used to create a list of names for your network. And these people can give you the names of others to contact.

Networking Worksheet — Friends List

Directions: How many friends do you have. Don't include just close friends, but include everyone who knows you by name and is friendly with you. Think hard and take a guess how many names of people you might be able to list in this list.

Write the number here: _____

Many people know more people than they realize. Use the following worksheet to list as many names of friends as you can think of. You can use additional pages later if you need more space. You also can add their phone numbers later.

Copyright © 1995 • JIST Works, Inc. • Indianapolis, IN 46202 • (317) 264-3720

Name	Phone Number
_____	_____
_____	_____
_____	_____
_____	_____
_____	_____
_____	_____
_____	_____
_____	_____
_____	_____
_____	_____
_____	_____
_____	_____
_____	_____
_____	_____
_____	_____
_____	_____
_____	_____
_____	_____
_____	_____
_____	_____
_____	_____
_____	_____
_____	_____
_____	_____
_____	_____
_____	_____

If you do the same thing for each of the groups on your list, you could end up with hundreds of names. Each one of these people knows other people. They would refer you to them if you asked. Then you would have many, many people in your job search network!

Copyright © 1995 • JIST Works, Inc. • Indianapolis, IN 46202 • (317) 264-3720

Cold Contacts — Making Direct Contacts with Employers

Contacting people you don't know is called cold contacting. The most common methods are using the phone to call an organization without being referred or dropping in without an appointment. Both of these methods are covered here.

Using the Yellow Pages to Make Cold Contacts

In any community, the very best list of organizations that might hire you is in the *Yellow Pages* of the phone book. It lists types of organizations all together by category.

This an easy way to find potential employers. And the telephone is an ideal way to contact these organizations. In one hour, you could call ten to twenty employers. With the right approach, you could set up one or more interviews in just that short period of time.

Use the Yellow Pages to Develop a Prospects List

You might be surprised at how many types of organizations could be sources of jobs for you. Here is how to do it:

Step 1: Find the Index

The *Yellow Pages* has an index in the front that lists the types of organizations in general groupings. They are arranged in alphabetical order.

Step 2: Select Likely Targets

Go through the index and, for each entry, ask yourself this question:

> *Could this type of organization use a person with my skills?*

If the answer is "yes" or "maybe," put a check by that type of organization.

Step 3: Prioritize Those Targets

For the types of organizations that you checked, put a number next to each based on how intersting it sounds to you. Use the following scale:

1 = Sounds very interesting
2 = Not sure if interested or not
3 = Does not sound interesting at all

Step 4: Call Specific Organizations

Once you have identified target groups, you can simply turn to the section of the *Yellow Pages* where those organizations are listed. Once there, you can use the phone numbers provided to phone them directly and ask for an interview. Although all this sounds easy, making effective phone calls takes practice. Chapter 9 will give you more information on how to use the phone to find job leads.

Copyright © 1995 • JIST Works, Inc. • Indianapolis, IN 46202 • (317) 264-3720

Create a list of Yellow Page Targets in an Organized Way

Take a look at the completed form that follows. The person was looking for a job as a secretary. The left column lists *Yellow Page* headings that could use a person with secretarial skills. In the column on the right, numbers are used to show how interested this person was in working for that type of organization.

This is a simple form and I have not included one in the book. You can use a sheet of paper to create your own similar form. Or you can simply identify the types of organizations to contact by writing in the *Yellow Pages* index itself. However you do it, this process is a good one to help you identify many job targets that you might otherwise overlook.

Yellow Pages Prospects Worksheet (Sample)

Position desired: _Secretary_

Types of Target Organizations	Level of interest*
1. Advertising	1
2. Airlines	2
3. Attorneys	2
4. Hospitals	3
5. Physicians	2
6. Insurance Companies	3
7. Television Stations	1
8. Banks	3
9. Sales Companies	1
10. Utilities	2

*   *1 = very*   *2 = somewhat*   *3 = not really, but possible*

Other Direct Contact Methods

If you look for them, there are many chances to make direct contacts with employers during your job search. Managers in many small organizations will see you if you just drop in. Even managers in large organizations will see you if you ask to see the person in charge.

Look for businesses that might use someone with your skills. Drop in and ask to see the person in charge. If this person is busy, ask when you should try again. Then call or go back. Usually, people are willing to see you — even on short notice.

Copyright © 1995 • JIST Works, Inc. • Indianapolis, IN 46202 • (317) 264-3720

Many times you can speak with the person in charge without an appointment. If so, tell them you are looking for a position and would like to speak with them briefly about your qualifications. If you're told they have no openings, say you would still like to talk about the possibility of future openings.

If they seem busy at this time, it is often best to set up a time when you can come back. Get a specific time and day for your appointment.

One of the most effective job search methods ever used is following up. Send a thank-you note after an interview. Arrange to call back at a certain date and time. Send a thank-you note after a helpful phone conversation with a member of your network. Stay in touch in a friendly and polite way with everyone on your network list.

In the last two chapters you learned the basic methods of finding a job:

✔ Use a variety of job-seeking methods.
✔ Get referrals and job leads from people who know you.
✔ Always try to make a direct contact with the person who will hire you.
✔ Follow up!

Copyright © 1995 • JIST Works, Inc. • Indianapolis, IN 46202 • (317) 264-3720

7

Filling Out Applications

Without Burying Yourself

Most large and some small employers require you to fill out an "application for employment" when you apply for a job. These forms collect information from you that an employer may need.

Why might an employer ask you to complete an application? List some of the reasons below.

Some Reasons Employers Use Applications

1. _____
2. _____
3. _____
4. _____
5. _____

Real Employers Use Applications

You probably listed several good reasons. But did you list that most employers use the application to screen out unqualified job seekers?

The major purpose of the application form is to help employers screen people out. If your qualifications are not "right" you will not get an interveiw.

Even qualified job seekers often get screened out based on their application form. It may have been eliminated because it was incomplete, had bad handwriting, or was messy. Some applicants get screened out because they did not have as much experience or as good "credentials" as others. Some employers screen out those who got paid more on their last job. There are many reasons for rejecting an applicant. You might be able to do that job, but you may never have the chance.

Completing an Application Is Not a Good Way to Get an Interview

Some people do get interviews by filling out an application. Many young people, for example, get their jobs in this way. This is because employers are often less selective for the entry-level and lower paying jobs often obtained in this way.

But filling out applications is not a very effective way to get an interview. As you have already learned, it is almost always better to ask an employer directly for an interview.

Even so, there are reasons that you should know how to successfully complete an application. Employers of larger organizations often require them. Even when you have already set up an interview in advance, some employers will ask you to complete an application before the interview. Goverment jobs require a completed application. And knowing how to complete an application can often help you prepare to answer some interview questions.

Copyright © 1995 • JIST Works, Inc. • Indianapolis, IN 46202 • (317) 264-3720

General Tips for Completing an Application

Here are some general suggestions for completing an application.

Follow Directions

Carefully read and complete all sections of the application. Follow the directions! If you are asked to print all responses, do not write! You can make a negative impression quickly if you don't follow directions.

Be Neat

A messy application will be rejected immediately. It will make you look as if you don't care. Carry an erasable black or blue ink pen with you for completing applications. These allow you to correct errors and are available at most department stores.

Provide Only Positive Information

Many application forms are designed to collect negative information. But if you provide it, it will be used to screen you out. Leaving a space blank is better than giving information that will keep you from being considered.

Use Any Available Space to Present Positive Information

For example, list any unpaid (volunteer) experience in the work experience section. List training you got in high school or the military that relates to the job you want. This is an exception to my earlier advice to follow the application's instructions. Find a place to put any helpful information, even if it is the margin!

Answering Problem Questions

Applications ask some difficult questions. How you answer them could get you screened out. Several laws now limit the types of questions an employer can ask on an application form or in an interview. Even so, some employers still use old application forms. These forms can ask "illegal" questions. If so, you can leave questions blank or simply draw a line through them.

Remember that you should never give negative information. Doing so will often result in your being screened out. But you should never lie on an application. That could get you fired later.

Copyright © 1995 • JIST Works, Inc. • Indianapolis, IN 46202 • (317) 264-3720

Let's review typical problem questions and ways to handle them.

Gaps in Employment

Employers like a complete history. They will wonder what you did during any times you were not employed. If you have a good reason for a gap in your employment history, be sure to list it. Say "raising children," "returned to school," or "helped uncle get a new business started." If you did anything for money during this time say "self-employed."

Did those activities relate in any way to the job you are looking for now? If so, present those skills you used and any accomplishments that might support your job objective.

If the employment gap was several years ago, simply show the start and finish dates of your employment as complete years. For example, 1995 to 1996 does not show any gap at all.

Arrest Record

Old applications used to ask "Have you ever been arrested?" New laws now allow an employer only to ask if you have ever been convicted of a serious crime such as a felony. Employers can also ask about crimes that could affect your ability to do the job. This allows some employers to ask about previous criminal records for child molesting, drug abuse, and other crimes.

These new laws are designed to keep you from being screened out of a job for arrests (when you were not found guilty) and minor crimes that would not affect your work. So, if you were ever arrested but not convicted of a felony, say "No" on the application.

Disabilities, Physical, or Emotional Problems

Unless your problem prevents you from doing the job safely, it is probably none of an employer's business. You should say "No" in almost all cases.

Reason for Leaving Last Job

Don't say "fired" if you were laid off because of a business slowdown or other good reason. Give the reason and make it sound positive. If you didn't leave on the best of terms but didn't do anything illegal, it is often best to list a legitimate excuse. Use something neutral such as "returned to school" or "decided on a career change." You can always explain the details in an interview.

Too Little Experience

If you don't have much experience for the job you want, emphasize your other strengths. Present any volunteer jobs in the work section and leave the wages paid blank. You can also give lots of details for any related training, education, and skills used in other jobs.

Copyright © 1995 • JIST Works, Inc. • Indianapolis, IN 46202 • (317) 264-3720

Pay Desired

Don't list a specific pay rate. It is often best to say "open" or "negotiable." This approach will not get you screened out.

Position Desired

If possible, list a broad career field. For example, say "general office" rather than a specific title, such as "secretary." Titles and duties are rarely the same from place to place.

Too Much or Too Little Education

If you are over qualified or your credentials are strong but in another field, consider leaving out some of your unrelated education. You may be applying for a job that usually requires advanced training or a degree. If you did not graduate, say you "attended" certain institutions. Don't say whether you did or did not graduate.

Let Your Conscience Be Your Guide

It should be clear that you could cross a line and start lying on an application. This is not a good idea. Many employers will later fire you if they find out you lied on your application. A better approach is to leave a sensitive question blank. If you have a serious problem that an application would reveal, you'll be better off looking for job openings that don't require an application.

The truth is, an application is more likely to do you harm than good. If you do fill one out, be sure that it is as good as you can make it. Include nothing that could get you screened out.

Sample Applications

I've included two sample applications in this chapter. The first one has been completed by the infamous Albert C. Smith and contains many errors. Find as many as you can and circle them. Then don't make the same mistakes on your own application!

 Next, for practice, use a pencil or erasable pen to complete the second blank application. Complete this application as carefully and as neatly as you can. Make sure all your dates, addresses, and other information are correct. When you're done, you can tear out this sample and take it with you on your job search. This is a very thorough application and it will provide all the details you will need (such as addresses and phone numbers) to complete most real applications.

Copyright © 1995 • JIST Works, Inc. • Indianapolis, IN 46202 • (317) 264-3720

APPLICATION
FOR EMPLOYMENT

PLEASE PRINT INFORMATION REQUESTED IN INK.

Date _April 1_

BROWN'S IS AN EQUAL OPPORTUNITY EMPLOYER and fully subscribes to the principles of Equal Employment Opportunity. Brown's has adopted an Affirmative Action Program to ensure that all applicants and employees are considered for hire, promotion and job status, without regard to race, color, religion, sex, national origin, age, handicap, or status as a disabled veteran or veteran of the Vietnam Era.

To protect the interests of all concerned, applicants for certain job assignment must pass a physical examination before they are hired.

Note: This application will be considered active for 90 days. If you have not been employed within this period and are still interested in employment at Brown's, please contact the office where you applied and request that your application be reactivated.

Name _Albert   C. Smith_   (Last First Middle)   Social Security Number _411-76-2614_
(Please present your Social Security Card for review.)

Address _1526 N. Otter_ (Number Street City State Zip Code)

County _Marion_   Current phone or nearest phone _____

Previous Address _Same_ (Number Street City State Zip Code)   Best time of day to contact _any_
(Answer only if position for which you are applying requires driving.)

If hired, can you furnish proof of age?   Yes ✔ No ____   Licensed to drive car?   Yes ___ No ___

If hired, can you furnish proof that you are legally entitled to work in U.S.?   Yes ✔ No ____   Is license valid in this state?   Yes ___ No ___

Have you ever been employed by Brown?   Yes ___ No ✗ If so, when ____ Position ____

Have you a relative in the employment of Brown's Department store?   Yes ___ No ✗

A PHYSICAL OR MENTAL DISABILITY WILL NOT CAUSE REJECTION IF IN BROWN'S MEDICAL OPINION YOU ARE ABLE TO SATISFACTORILY PERFORM IN THE POSITION FOR WHICH YOU ARE BEING CONSIDERED. Alternative placement, if available, of an applicant who does not meet the physical standards of the job for which he/she was originally considered is permitted.

Do you have any physical or mental impairment which may limit your ability to perform the job for which you are applying? _Yes, I have a back problem and was in Central State Hospital for 6 months._

If yes, what can reasonably be done to accommodate your limitation? ____

	School Attended	No. of Years	Name of School	City/State	Graduate?	Course or College Major	Average Grades
EDUCATION	Grammar	6	Holy Trinity	Scranton	Yes	General	B
	Jr. High	3	Crestview	" "	" "	" "	B
	Sr. High	3	WCHS	" "	" "	" "	B
	Other					College Prep	
	College	3	State U	Scranton	No	Degree	C

	BRANCH OF SERVICE	DATE ENTERED	SERVICE DATE OF DISCHARGE	HIGHEST RANK HELD	SERVICE-RELATED SKILLS AND EXPERIENCE APPLICABLE TO CIVILIAN EMPLOYMENT
MILITARY SERVICE	USA	1987	1990	E-3	radio stuff

What experience or training have you had other than your work experience, military service and education? (Community activities, hobbies, etc.) _I take things apart and fix them._

I am interested in the type of work I have checked:

Sales ✗   Office ✔   Mechanical ✗   Warehouse ✔   Other (Specify) _Various_

Or the following specific Job _anything_

I am seeking (check only one):

✔ Temporary employment (6 days or less)

✔ Seasonal employment (one season, e.g., Christmas)

✔ Regular employment (employment for indifinite period of time)

I am available for (check only one)

✔ Part-Time

✗ Full-Time   Work

If part-time, indicate maximum hours per week ____ and enter hours available in block to the right.

If temporary, indicate dates available ____

Have you been convicted during the past seven years of a serious crime involving a person's life or property?

NO ✗   YES ✗   If yes, explain: _drunk in public_

HOURS AVAILABLE FOR WORK

Sun.	To
Mon.	To
Tues.	To
Wed.	_anytime_ To
Thurs.	To
Fri.	To
Sat.	To

Copyright © 1995 • JIST Works, Inc. • Indianapolis, IN 46202 • (317) 264-3720

REFERENCES

LIST BELOW YOUR FOUR MOST RECENT EMPLOYERS, BEGINNING WITH THE CURRENT OR MOST RECENT ONE. IF YOU HAVE HAD LESS THAN FOUR EMPLOYERS, USE THE REMAINING SPACES FOR PERSONAL REFERENCES IF YOU WERE EMPLOYED UNDER A MAIDEN OR OTHER NAME. PLEASE ENTER THAT NAME IN THE RIGHT HAND MARGIN. IF APPLICABLE, ENTER SERVICE IN THE ARMED FORCES ON THE REVERSE SIDE.

NAMES AND ADDRESSES OF FORMER EMPLOYERS, BEGINNING WITH THE CURRENT OR MOST RECENT	Nature of Employer's Business	Name of your Supervisor	What kind of work did you do?	Starting Date	Starting Pay	Date of Leaving	Pay at Leaving	Why did you leave? Give details
NOTE: State reason for and length of inactivity between present application date and last employer.			*I would rather not say*					
Name *J.P.J* Tel. No.	*School*	*Eric Burgess*	*clean up*	Month ? '92 Year Per Week	*$6 an hr*	Month 3 Year Per Week	*$6*	*Fired—but it wasn't my fault*
Address *Walnut St.* Zip Code								
City *Scranton* State *PA*								
NOTE: State reason for and length of inactivity between last employer and second employer. *Looked for a job — almost a year*								
Name *Fred Willis* Tel. No. ?	*Houses*	*Rafael something*	*electrician helper labor*	Month 8 '90 Year Per Week	*$7 an hr*	Month 10 Year Per Week	*$7*	*boss always picked on me*
Address *don't know* Zip Code								
City *Scranton* State *PA*								
NOTE: State reason for and length of inactivity between second last employer and third last employer. *Looked for a job*								
Name *Wayne Const.* Tel. No. *555-4141*	*Construction staff*	*Mark Henoki*	*Jack hammer wiring*	Month 6 '85 Year Per Week	*$5.75*	Month 4 '86 Year Per Week	*$6*	*Company went broke*
Address *436 N. Anderson* Zip Code								
City *Scranton* State *PA*								
NOTE: State reason for and length of inactivity between third last employer and fourth last employer. *couldn't find work*								
Name *Central State Hospital* Tel. No.	*mental hospital*	*Lynn Donovan*	*clean up*	Month ? '94 Year Per Week	*$4.20 hr*	Month 7 '94 Year Per Week	*none*	*I got better and was discharged*
Address *Washington St.* Zip Code								
City *Scranton* State *PA*								

I certify that the information in this application is correct to the best of my knowledge and understand that any misstatement or omission of information is grounds for dismissal in accordance with Brown's policy. I authorize the references listed above to give you any and all information concerning my previous employment and any pertinent information they may have, personal or otherwise, and release all parties from all liability for any damage that may result from furnishing same to you. In consideration of my employment, I agree to conform to the rules and regulations of Browns, and my employment and compensation can be terminated with or without cause, and with or without notice, at any time, at the option of either the Company or myself. I understand that no unit manager or representative of Brown's other than the President or Vice-President of the Company, has any authority to enter into any agreement for employment for any specified period of time, or to make any agreement contrary to the foregoing. In some states, the law requires that Brown's have my written permission before obtaining consumer reports on me, and I hereby authorize Brown's to obtain such reports.

Applicant's Signature *Smith, Albert C.*

NOT TO BE FILLED OUT BY APPLICANT

INTERVIEWER'S COMMENTS	Date of Empl.		Tested		(Store will enter dates as required.)		Mailed	Completed
I really need a job now.	Dept. or Div.	Regular ____ Part-Time ____	Physical examination scheduled for *last year*		REFERENCE REQUESTS		*not yet*	
	Job Title		Physical examination form completed *didn't get one*		CONSUMER REPORT			
	Job Title Code	Job Grade	Review Card prepared	Minor's Work Permit	Withholding Tax (W-4)			
	Compensation Arrangement *make me an offer*		Timecard prepared	Proof of Birth	State Withholding Tax			
	Manager Approving			Training Material Given to Employee				
Prospect for	Employee No.	Rack No.	Unit Name and Number *Albert Smith*					
1.								
2.								

DATE: _____

JIST's Application for Employment
(PLEASE PRINT REQUESTED INFORMATION IN INK.)

JIST Works, Inc. is an Equal Opportunity Employer and does not discriminate against any individual in any phase of employment in accordance with the requirements of local, state, and federal law. In addition, JIST has adopted an Affirmative Action Program with the goal of ensuring equitable representation of qualified women, minorities, Vietnam Era and disabled veterans, and other disabled individuals at all job levels.

Applicants may be subject to testing for illegal drugs. In addition, applicants for certain positions that receive a conditional offer of employment must pass a medical examination or meet other criteria prior to receiving a confirmed offer of employment.

PERSONAL INFORMATION

LAST NAME	FIRST NAME	MIDDLE INITIAL	SOCIAL SECURITY NO.

STREET ADDRESS OR RFD NO. (include apartment no., if any)	HOW LONG AT THIS ADDRESS?

CITY	STATE/PROVINCE	COUNTY/PARISH	ZIP CODE

HOME PHONE (include area code)	WORK PHONE (include area code) Ext.	SEX (for statistics only) ❑ Male ❑ Female	Other Last Names Ever Used

PREVIOUS ADDRESS (if less than one year)	HOW LONG AT THIS ADDRESS?

CITY	STATE/PROVINCE	COUNTY/PARISH	ZIP CODE

POSITION APPLIED FOR:

I AM AVAILABLE FOR: ❑ Part-time ❑ Full-time
Complete the Hours Available for Work chart below.

HOW DID YOU HEAR OF THIS OPENING?

	Sun.	Mon.	Tues.	Wed.	Thurs.	Fri.	Sat.
FROM							
TO							

LOWEST RATE OF PAY YOU WILL ACCEPT:

WHEN WILL YOU BE AVAILABLE FOR WORK? (month and year)

ARE YOU AVAILABLE FOR TEMPORARY EMPLOYMENT?

	YES	NO
A. Less than 1 month?		
B. 1 to 4 months?		
C. 5 to 12 months?		

IF HIRED, CAN YOU FURNISH PROOF OF AGE?
❑ Yes ❑ No

IF HIRED, CAN YOU FURNISH PROOF THAT YOU ARE LEGALLY ENTITLED TO WORK IN THE U.S.?
❑ Yes ❑ No

Answer the following only if the position for which you are applying requires driving.
Are you licensed to drive a car? ❑ Yes ❑ No Is license valid in this state? ❑ Yes ❑ No

HAVE YOU EVER BEEN BONDED? ❑ No   ❑ Yes - When

DO YOU HAVE ANY PHYSICAL HANDICAPS PREVENTING YOU FROM DOING CERTAIN TYPES OF WORK?
❑ No   ❑ Yes If Yes, describe handicap/limitations.

HAVE YOU HAD ANY SERIOUS ILLNESS IN THE PAST 5 YEARS? ❑ No   ❑ Yes If Yes, describe.

Please list any special skills, training, or experiences which qualify you for the position for which you are applying.

_____

_____

_____

Please list any additional qualifications and skills (skills with machines, patents or inventions, your most important publication [do not submit copies unless requested], your public speaking and publications experience, membership in professional or scientific societies, etc.)

_____

Kind of license or certificate (pilot, registered nurse, lawyer, radio operator, CPA, etc.):	Latest license or certificate: Year	State or other licensing authority	Approximate number of words per minute: Typing	Shorthand

Copyright © 1995 • JIST Works, Inc. • Indianapolis, IN 46202 • (317) 264-3720

EDUCATION

Did you graduate from high school or will you graduate within the next nine months, or do you have a GED high school equivalency certificate?	Name and location (city and state) of last high school attended:
❏ Yes, month/year ❏ No, highest grade completed:	

Name and location (city, state, ZIP code, if known) of college or university. (If you expect to graduate within nine months give MONTH and YEAR you expect to receive your degree.)	Dates Attended		No. of Credits Completed		Type of Degree (e.g. B.A.)	Year of Degree	GPA
	From	To	Semester Hours	Quarter Hours			

Chief undergraduate college subjects:	No. of Credits Completed		Chief graduate college subjects:	No. of Credits Completed	
	Semester	Quarter		Semester	Quarter

Major field of study at highest level of college work:

Other schools or training (for example, trade, vocational, Armed Forces or business). Give for each the name and location (city, state, and Zip code, if known) of school, dates attended, subjects studied, number of classroom hours of instruction per week, certificate, and any other pertinent data.

_____

_____

_____

Activities, honors, awards, and fellowships received:

Languages other than English. List the languages (other than English) in which you are proficient and indicate your level of proficiency by putting an (X) in the appropriate columns.

	PROFICIENCY							
	Can Prepare and Deliver Lectures		Can Converse		Have Facility to Translate Articles, Tech. Materials, etc.		Can Read Articles, Technical Materials, for Own Use	
Name of Language	Fluently	With Difficulty	Fluently	Passably	Into English	From English	Easily	With Difficulty

REFERENCES

List three persons who are NOT related to you and who have definite knowledge of your qualifications and fitness for the position for which you are applying. Do not repeat names of supervisors listed under EXPERIENCE.

Full Name	Present Business or Home Address (Number, Street, City, State, and ZIP Code)	Telephone Number (Include Area Code)	Business or Occupation

NOTE: A conviction or a firing does not necessarily mean you cannot be appointed. The circumstances of the occurance(s) and how long ago it (they) occurred are important. Give all the facts so that a decision can be made.

	YES	NO
1. Within the last five years have you been fired from any job for any reason?		
2. Within the last five years have you quit a job after being notified you would be fired?		

    If your answer to questions 1 and 2 is "YES," give details in the space provided on the following page. Show the name and address (including ZIP Code) of employer, approximate date, and reasons in each case. This information should agree with your answers under EXPERIENCE.

	YES	NO

3. Have you ever been convicted, forfeited collateral, or are you now under charges for any felony or any firearms or explosives offense against the law? (A felony is defined as any offense punishable by imprisonment for a term exceeding one year, but does not include any offense under the laws of a state as a misdemeanor. ....

4. During the past seven years, have you been convicted, imprisoned, on probation or parole, or forfeited collateral, or are you now under charges for any offense against the law not included in the above question? ....

NOTE: *When answering the previous two questions, you may omit (1) traffic fines for which you paid a fine of $100.00 or less, (2) any offense committed before your 18th birthday which was finally adjudicated in a juvenile court or under a youth offender law, (3) any conviction the record of which has been expunged under federal or state law, and (4) any conviction set aside under the Federal Youth Corrections Act or similar state authority.*

PERSONAL REFERENCES

NAME	ADDRESS	RELATIONSHIP	PHONE NUMBER

LIST ONLY PERSONS WE MAY CONTACT — BE SURE TO INCLUDE PHONE NUMBER

	YES	NO

5. While in the military service, were you ever convicted by a general court-martial? ....
   If your answer to questions 3, 4 or 5 is "YES," give details in the space below. Show for each offense, (1) date; (2) charge; (3) place; (4) court; (5) action taken.

6. Do you receive, or do you have pending, application for retirement or retainer pay, pension, or other compensation based upon military, federal, civilian, or District of Columbia government service? ....
   If your answer to this question is "YES," give details below. If military retired pay, include the rank at which you retired.

Your statemet cannot be processed until you have answered all questions, including questions 1 through 6 above.

QUESTION #	SPACE FOR DETAILED ANSWERS. BE SURE TO INDICATE QUESTION NUMBER TO WHICH THE ANSWERS APPLY.

If more space is required, use full sheets of paper approximately the same size as this page. Write on each sheet your name, birth date, and announcement or position title. Attach all sheets to this page.

VETERAN PREFERENCES

Answer all parts. If a part does not apply to you, answer "No."

	YES	NO

Have you ever served on active duty in the United States military service? (Exclude tours of active duty for training in the Reserve or National Guard) ....

Have you ever been discharged from the armed services under other than honorable conditions? (You may omit any such discharge changed to honorable or general by a Discharge Review Board or similar authority) ....

If the above answer is "YES," you will be required to furnish records to support your claim at the time you are hired.

List dates, branch, and serial number of all active service (enter N/A, if not applicable).

FROM	TO	BRANCH OF SERVICE	SERIAL OR SERVICE NUMBER	

BRANCH	RANK	DUTIES	SALARY FROM	TO	REASON FOR CHANGE IN RANK

List any special school or skills acquired during your military service:

Copyright © 1995 • JIST Works, Inc. • Indianapolis, IN 46202 • (317) 264-3720

EXPERIENCE

Begin with current or most recent job or volunteer experience and work back. Account for periods of unemployment exceeding three months and your residence address at that time on the last line of the experience blocks in order of occurrence.

May inquiry be made of your present employer regarding your character qualifications and record of employment   ❑ Yes   ❑ No

1. NAME AND ADDRESS OF EMPLOYER'S ORGANIZATION

Dates employed (month/year)		Average number of hours per week	Salary or earnings	
From	To		Start$	per
			End $	per

Exact title of your position	Name of immediate supervisor	Area Code Phone Number	Number and kind of employees you supervised

Kind of business or organization (manufacturing, accounting, social services, etc.) | Reason for leaving

Description of work. (Describe your specific duties, responsibilities and accomplishments in this job.)

_____

_____

_____

_____

2. NAME AND ADDRESS OF EMPLOYER'S ORGANIZATION

Dates employed (month/year)		Average number of hours per week	Salary or earnings	
From	To		Start$	per
			End $	per

Exact title of your position	Name of immediate supervisor	Area Code Phone Number	Number and kind of employees you supervised

Kind of business or organization (manufacturing, accounting, social services, etc.) | Reason for leaving

Description of work. (Describe your specific duties, responsibilities and accomplishments in this job.)

_____

_____

_____

_____

3. NAME AND ADDRESS OF EMPLOYER'S ORGANIZATION

Dates employed (month/year)		Average number of hours per week	Salary or earnings	
From	To		Start$	per
			End $	per

Exact title of your position	Name of immediate supervisor	Area Code Phone Number	Number and kind of employees you supervised

Kind of business or organization (manufacturing, accounting, social services, etc.) | Reason for leaving

Description of work. (Describe your specific duties, responsibilities and accomplishments in this job.)

_____

_____

_____

_____

ATTENTION — THIS STATEMENT MUST BE SIGNED
Read the following paragraphs carefully before signing this statement.

The information provided by me in this application for employment is true and complete to the best of my knowledge. I understand that if I am employed, any false statements will be considered as cause for possible dismissal. You are hereby authorized to conduct any investigation of my personal history and/or credit and financial records employing investigative or credit agencies or bureaus of your choice subject to the provisions of the Fair Credit Reporting Act.

_____   _____
Signature of applicant (sign in ink)   Date

APPLICANT — DO NOT WRITE IN THIS SECTION

INTERVIEWER	DATE	COMMENTS		
DEPARTMENT	POSITION	WILL REPORT	LOCATION	SALARY
APPROVED: PERSONNEL DEPARTMENT	DEPARTMENT MANAGER		GENERAL MANAGER	

Copyright © 1995 • JIST Works, Inc. • Indianapolis, IN 46202 • (317) 264-3720

JIST Cards

Your Personal Calling Card

magine that you are an employer and can hire someone for a position in an auto shop. You may or may not have a job opening now. Read the card below and then answer the questions that follow it.

John Kijek

Home: (219) 232-9213
Message: (219) 637-6643

Position Desired: Auto mechanic

Skills: Over three years work experience including one year in a full-time auto mechanic's training program. Familiar with all hand tools and electronic diagnostic equipment. Can handle common auto repair tasks such as tune ups, brakes, exhaust systems, electrical and mechanical repairs. Am a fast worker, often completing jobs correctly in less than the standard time. Have all tools required to start working immediately.

- Prefer full-time work, any shift
- Honest, reliable, good with people

Copyright © 1995 • JIST Works, Inc. • Indianapolis, IN 46202 • (317) 264-3720

How Did You React?

Directions: *Please answer these questions. Be truthful. Base your answers on your reaction to the information on the card.*

1. Do you feel good about this person? (yes or no) _____
2. What were your emotions about this person, how did you feel about him? _____
   _____
   _____

3. Would you be willing to interview him if you had a job opening? (yes or no)_____
   Why? _____
   _____
   _____

4. Would you be willing to see him even if you did not have a job opening? (yes or no) _____
   Why? _____
   _____
   _____

It's a JIST Card

What you read on the previous page is a JIST Card. JIST stands for Job Information and Seeking Training. It is a name used to identify a whole series of job search techniques I began to develop in the early 1970s. Many of those techniques are included in this book. With more than 20 years of research and improvement, these job search techniques are among the most effective ever developed.

Most people can read a JIST Card in fewer than 30 seconds. Yet in that very short period of time, the JIST Card often creates a positive impression! In fact, most people who read it say they would interview such a person based on just this much information.

JIST Cards are the only job search tool that are able to create such an impresssion — and get interviews — in such a short period of time. They are a new and effective job search tool that can become very important to you.

Copyright © 1995 • JIST Works, Inc. • Indianapolis, IN 46202 • (317) 264-3720

How You Can Use a JIST Card

A JIST Card is a 3" x 5" index card you can use in many ways. It is similar to a mini-resume or business calling card. JIST Cards are usually inexpensively printed at a print shop so you will have plenty to use during your job search.

Some Uses for Your JIST Card

- Attach it to a completed application.
- Give it to a friend or relative. Ask them to keep you in mind if they hear of any job openings. And ask them to give the card to someone else who might know of a job.
- Send one to an employer before an interview.
- Enclose one in your thank-you note after an interview or phone contact.
- Give several to people who are willing to give them to others. Everyone in your network groups should get some. Ask them to give them to others who might know of a job opening for you.
- Attach one to a resume.

You may have other ideas on how to use them. For example, they have been put on grocery store bulletin boards, under car windshield wiper blades in parking lots, and used in other creative ways. The more you can put into use, the better!

Copyright © 1995 • JIST Works, Inc. • Indianapolis, IN 46202 • (317) 264-3720

The Anatomy of a JIST Card

There is more to a well-written JIST Card than it might seem. Look over the different sections of a JIST Card in the sample below. Additional details on each section also are provided following the card itself.

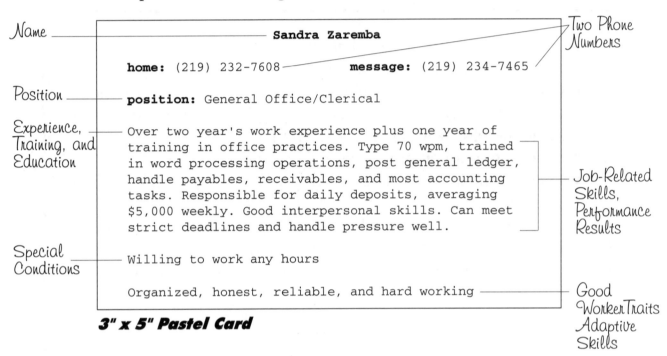

Name — Sandra Zaremba

home: (219) 232-7608   **message:** (219) 234-7465

Two Phone Numbers

Position — **position:** General Office/Clerical

Experience, Training, and Education — Over two year's work experience plus one year of training in office practices. Type 70 wpm, trained in word processing operations, post general ledger, handle payables, receivables, and most accounting tasks. Responsible for daily deposits, averaging $5,000 weekly. Good interpersonal skills. Can meet strict deadlines and handle pressure well.

Job-Related Skills, Performance Results

Special Conditions — Willing to work any hours

Organized, honest, reliable, and hard working — *Good Worker Traits Adaptive Skills*

3" x 5" Pastel Card

The Parts of a JIST Card

A JIST Card is small, so it can't contain many details. But consider what John Kijek's card does include:

Identification: John's name is given.

A Way to Contact Him: John lists two phone numbers. An employer will almost always phone rather than send a letter. By giving the number of a reliable friend or answering service who will take messages, John can always be reached.

Length of Experience: John listed his total length of work experience with his skills. He included his auto mechanic training where he developed some skills and learned to be a hard worker. He can describe this experience in the job interview, along with his informal experience working on cars as a hobby.

Related Education and Training: John listed training with his experience to give a longer total of work and training time. A person with more experience could list related education or training separately.

Copyright © 1995 • JIST Works, Inc. • Indianapolis, IN 46202 • (317) 264-3720

Skills: This section tells what John can do and how well he can do it. These are job-related skills. John also mentions an important transferable skill — he is fast and thorough in his work.

Preferred Working Conditions: John has listed two preferences for the type of work he wants. Both of these are positives.

Good Worker Traits: John lists adaptive skills and traits that would be important to most employers.

All this in fewer than 30 seconds!

Sample JIST Cards

Following are some sample JIST Cards. Study them and use any ideas that help you with your own card. While you can type or even handwrite your own cards, several of the samples have been done on a word-processing computer and printed on a laser printer. These will show you some of the simple but effective formats that can be done on these systems.

Jonathan McLaughlin   Home/Answering Machine: (509) 674-8736

Objective: Electronics — installation, maintenance & sales

SKILLS: Four years work experience plus two years advanced training in electronics. AS degree in Electronics Engineering Technology. Managed a $500,000/yr. business while going to school full time, with grades in the top 25%. Familiar with all major electronics diagnostic and repair equipment. Hands-on experience with medical, consumer, communications, business, and industrial electronics equipment and applications. Good problem-solving and communication skills. Customer service oriented.

Willing to do what it takes to get the job done.

Self-motivated, dependable, learn quickly

Maria Marquez

Home: (213) 432-8064   Messages: (213) 437-9836

Position Desired: Hotel Management

Four years experience in sales, catering, and accounting in 300-room hotel. Associate's degree in Hotel Management plus one year with the Bouleau Culinary Institute. Doubled revenues from meetings and conferences. Increased dining room and bar revenues by 44%. Have been commended for improving staff productivity and courtesy. I approach my work with hard work, imagination, and creative problem-solving skills.

Enthusiastic, well-organized, detail-oriented

Jessica Bruisehard
Home (846) 387-9838
Answering Service: (846) 238-9845

Objective: Business management position requiring skills in problem solving, planning, organizing and cost management.

Skills: BA Degree in business management and over ten years of management experience in progressively responsible positions. Responsible for as many as 40 staff and budgets in excess of $6 million. Consistent record of getting results. Excellent communication skills. Thorough knowledge of budgeting, cost savings, computerized data base, word processing, and spreadsheet programs. Enjoy challenges and accept responsibility.

Willing to relocate

Results-oriented, good problem-solving skills, energetic

Dennis Franz

Job Objective: Building, Grounds, and Equipment Maintenance

Skills: Four years plant management experience plus related military training. Supervised over 200,000 square feet in industrial and warehouse facilities and 8 staff. Reorganized workloads so that retiring full-time staff could be replaced by part-time workers from a local technical school, saving over $30,000 a year in expenses. Implemented an energy saving program that reduced energy costs by over $70,000 per year. I take pride in operating a clean, safe, and efficient operation.

Can work any hours

Well-organized, problem solver, willing to relocate

Copyright © 1995 • JIST Works, Inc. • Indianapolis, IN 46202 • (317) 264-3720

JIST Card Worksheet

Directions: *This worksheet provides lots of instructions for writing your own JIST Card. Read the instructions carefully, then complete each section of the worksheet as well as you can. Later, you can take this information and use it to write your final draft.*

Your Name: _____

Tips: Keep it simple. Don't use nicknames, middle names, or initials if possible.

Phone Number: _____

Alternate Phone Number: _____

Tips: You can use one phone number if you use an answering machine at home and you always leave it on when you are not there. If you don't have a home phone, get permission to use a friend's or relative's or use theirs as a back up. Make sure that your phone will be answered profesionally at all times (no silly answering machine messages, for example). Anyone who might answer it needs to know how to take accurate messages. Always include your area code.

Job Objective: _____

_____

_____

Tips: Don't be too narrow in your job objective. Say "general office" rather than "receptionist" if you would consider a variety of office jobs. If you are more narrow in your job objective, try to avoid a job title but give other details. For example, say "Management position in an insurance-related business," or "Working with children in a medical or educational setting."
Don't limit yourself to entry-level jobs if you have potential or interest in doing more. If you say "Office Manager" instead of "secretary," you just might get it. If you are not too sure of your ability to get a higher-paying job, it is still best to keep your options open if possible. Say "Office manager or responsible secretarial position," for example.

Work Experience

Directions: *Writing your experience statement is a tricky matter for some people. To help you with this important statement, I have included lots of tips. The first set of tips will help you complete the box below. Read those tips before completing the entries in the box.*

Your Total Experience

Write either years or months (if you don't have much experience) in the spaces beside each question.

a.   Total of paid work _____

b.   Total of volunteer work + _____

c.   Total of informal work + _____

d.   Total of related education or training = _____

Copyright © 1995 • JIST Works, Inc. • Indianapolis, IN 46202 • (317) 264-3720

Tips for completing Your Total Experience

There are several things to consider in writing your JIST Card's experience statement. You want to take advantage of all the experience you have that supports your job objective. If you are changing careers, have been out of the work world for awhile, or do not have very much work experience, you will need to use other experiences to convince the employer you can do the job.

Depending on your situation, you can include any or all of the following as part of your work experience.

Paid Work: You can list any work you were paid to do. The work does not have to be similar to the job you are looking for now. Baby-sitting and lawn mowing jobs count. So can working in a fast-food place. If you worked part time, estimate the number of hours you worked. Divide this total number of hours by 160 hours to get the number of months you worked. Of course, paid work that is directly related to your job objective is the best, if you have it.

Volunteer Work: You can include volunteer work as part of your total work experience. It does count, and you should do this if you don't have much paid work experience.

Informal Work: Include work you did at home or as an unpaid hobby. It is best if this work relates to the job, but it doesn't have to. For example, if you worked on cars at home and want to be an auto mechanic, there is an obvious connection. You may have experience taking care of younger brothers or sisters. Or working in the family business. This is real experience and, if it can help you to use it, do so.

Related Education and Training: If you took business courses in high school or college and want to work in accounting, those courses are part of your experience. So are any courses or training you received in the military, in college, business or technical school, or anywhere else. If they relate in some way to the job you want, they can count.

Tips for Writing Your Experience Statement

Because everyone has a different background, no single rule can be given for everyone. Here are some tips for writing your own experience statement.

If you have lots of work experience: If part of this experience is not related, you can leave it out. If you have 20 years of experience, say "Over 15" or include just the experience that directly relates to this job. This keeps the employer from knowing how old you are. Your age is an advantage you will present in the interview!

If you don't have much paid work experience: You need to include everything possible. If you have no paid work experience related to the job you now

94

Copyright © 1995 • JIST Works, Inc. • Indianapolis, IN 46202 • (317) 264-3720

seek, emphasize your education, training, and other work. For example, "Nearly two years of experience including one year of advanced training in office procedures."

Remember to include the total of all paid and unpaid work as part of your experience! Include all those part-time jobs by saying "Over 18 months total work experience. . ."

If your experience is in another field: Just mention that you have "Four years work experience," without saying in what.

Other: If you won promotions, raises, or have other special strengths, this is certainly the time to say so. "Over seven years of increasingly responsible work experience, including three years as a supervisor. Promoted twice."

 Directions: *Look over the sample JIST Cards for additional ideas, then write your own statement below.*

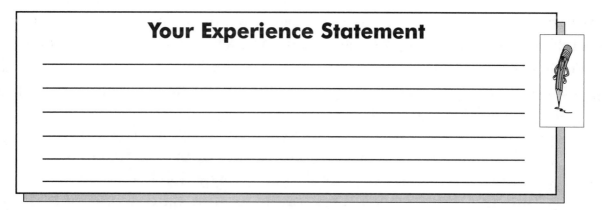

Your Experience Statement

Education and Training

Depending on your situation, you can combine your education and training with your experience. This is done in several of the sample JIST Cards and in one of the experience statements just discussed. Or you can list your education and training as a separate statement.

Don't mention your education or training at all if it doesn't help you. If you have a license, certification, or degree that supports your job objective, you may want to mention it here, too. For example: "Four years of experience plus two years of training leading to certification as an Emergency Medical Technician."

Look over the sample JIST Cards for more ideas and write your own education and training statement on the next page. If you want, you can also revise your previous experience statement to include your education and training, and include your new statement on the next page.

Your Education and Training Statement

_____

_____

_____

_____

_____

_____

Skills Section

In this section you list the things you can do. If appropriate, mention any job-related tools or equipment you can use. Use the language of the job to describe the more important things you can do. It is best to use some numbers to strengthen what you say and to emphasize results. Instead of saying "Skills include typing, dictation, (and so on)," say "Accurately type 80 words per minute and am familiar with major word processing software on PC and Mac computers."

Emphasize results! It is too easy to overlook the importance of what you do. Add up the numbers of transactions you handled, the money you were responsible for, the results you got. Some examples:

- A person with fast food experience might write "Have handled over 50,000 customer contacts with total sales of over $250,000 quickly and accurately." While many think that a "lowly" job like those in fast-food are not worthy jobs, they often require hard work, speed, and advanced skills. The figures used here are based on a five-day week, 200 customers a day for one year, and an average sale of $5. Impressive numbers, when presented in this way. And the fact that this was done in a fast-food job does not have to be mentioned.

- Someone who ran a small store could say "Responsible for business with over $150,000 in sales per year. Increased sales by 35% within 18 months."

- You could present a successful school fund-raising project as: "Planned, trained, and supervised a staff of six on a special project. Exceeded income projections by 40%."

You should also include one or more of your transferable skills that are important for that job.

- A receptionist might add "Good appearance and pleasant telephone voice." It is certainly OK to give numbers to support these skills, too!

- A warehouse manager might say "Well organized and efficient. Have reduced expenses by 20% while orders increased by 55%."

Copyright © 1995 • JIST Works, Inc. • Indianapolis, IN 46202 • (317) 264-3720

Directions: Look over the sample JIST Cards and write your own statement below.

Your Skills Statement

_____

_____

_____

_____

_____

_____

_____

_____

_____

_____

_____

Preferred Working Conditions

This is an optional section. You can add just a few words — one or two lines at most — to let the employer know what you are willing to do. Do not limit your employment possibilities by saying "Will only work days" or "No travel wanted." It is better to leave this blank than give anything negative.

Directions: Look at the sample JIST Cards for ideas. Then write your own statement below.

Your Preferred Working Conditions Statement

_____

_____

_____

Good Worker Skills

Directions: List three or four of your key adaptive skills. Choose skills that are most important in the job you are seeking. Be certain you do have them! Refer to chapter 3 for your list of adaptive skills as needed. The sample JIST Cards also will give you ideas. Then list the skills you will include on your own JIST Card on the next page.

Copyright © 1995 • JIST Works, Inc. • Indianapolis, IN 46202 • (317) 264-3720

Your Adaptive Skills and Good Worker Traits

_____

_____

_____

The Final Edit

To fit all this information on a 3" x 5" card, you will probably need to edit what you've written. Here are some tips to help you write your final version:

- Make every word count in your final version. Get rid of anything that does not directly support your job objective.

- Use short, choppy sentences. You don't have to use complete sentences. Remember, every word has to count, so cut any words that are not necessary.

- Add more information if your JIST Card is too short. But add things only if it makes your statements stronger.

- Cut anything that is not a positive. Get rid of anything that does not present you in a positive way.

- Handwrite or print it on a 3" x 5" card. This will help you see if you have included too much or too little. Edit it again as needed to make it fit.

- Read your JIST Card out loud. This will help you to know how it sounds and may give you additional ideas to improve it.

- Ask someone else to help you with the final version. He or she may make some good suggestions for you to consider, but make your own final decisions.

- Check it one more time. Make sure your final version does not have any misspelling or other errors in it. One error can create a negative impression and undo all your hard work!

JIST Card Production Tips

Here are a few tips for getting your JIST Card produced in its final form.

- You want to put lots of JIST Cards in circulation. While you can type or even handwrite individual JIST Cards, it is best to have them printed in quantities of at least 100 to 500.

Copyright © 1995 • JIST Works, Inc. • Indianapolis, IN 46202 • (317) 264-3720

- You can use a good qualilty typewriter to create your original JIST Card. But it is usually much better to have them professionally word processed on a computer. If you don't have access to a computer and good laser printer, you can get this done at most print shops for a modest fee.

- Computer generated JIST Cards also have the advantage of allowing you to use different type sizes and styles, as well as interesting graphic elements such as lines. You also can squeeze more content onto your card by using a smaller type size.

- Just to be sure that no new errors were introduced in the final version, edit it once more. Make sure that the phone numbers are correct (errors have been made!) and that no new typographical errors have crept in.

- You can fit five copies of the same JIST Card on one standard sheet of 8 1/2" x 11" paper. Doing this allows you to copy or print multiple sheets in the most efficient way. Of course, you will need to cut the sheets down to the correct size of the individual cards.

- Use "light card stock," not paper, for your JIST Cards. It is the same thickness used for a standard 3" x 5" card. Office supply stores often carry it in a range of colors in standard 8 1/2" x 11" size paper that will work in most copy machines.

- I like off-white, ivory, or cream-color JIST Cards, as they give the cards a professional appearance. You can use other light pastel colors such as blue, gray, and others. For most purposes, I do not suggest the use of pink, red, or green — though you can use them if it is important for you to do so.

- A good quality photocopy machine can print copies of your JIST Cards. Make sure that the copy quality is excellent and that it will handle what is called "light card stock" without jamming. Computer laser printers also can be used to print final copies of your JIST Cards.

- Most good print shops also can print your JIST Cards (and resumes) on high quality printing equipment. They usually have a selection of card stock and paper that can be used for this. They may also have matching paper to give you a coordinated look for your resumes, JIST Cards, thank-you notes, and envelopes.

- Look in the *Yellow Pages* of the phone book for sources of printing and word processing under headings such as Printers, Resume Service, Typing Service, and Secretarial Services. Call in advance and ask for approximate prices for what you need to have done.

■ You will often save time and money by having your resume and JIST Card prepared at the same time. But do this only if writing your resume does not delay the start of your job search — and distribution of your JIST Cards. Resumes will be covered later in this book.

Use Your JIST Cards!

Once you have your JIST Cards, use them! Give them away freely because they will not help you get a job if they sit on your desk. The more you have in circulation, the more people know about you and your skills. Try them, they work.

Copyright © 1995 • JIST Works, Inc. • Indianapolis, IN 46202 • (317) 264-3720

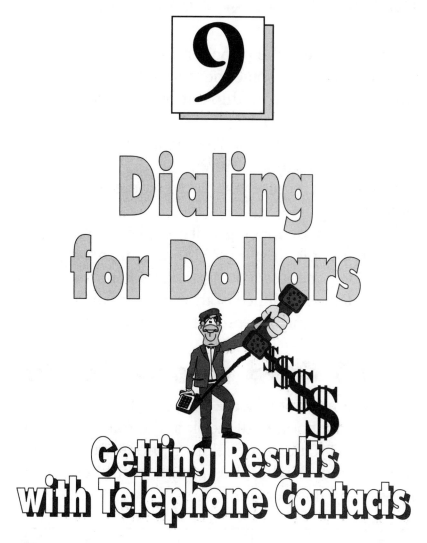

9

Dialing for Dollars

Getting Results with Telephone Contacts

*U*sing the telephone is one of the most efficient ways of looking for work. You don't spend time traveling, and you can talk to large numbers of people in a very short time. In one morning, for example, you can easily talk to more than 20 employers — once you learn how.

In fact, many job seekers get more interviews by using the phone than with any other method. You can call people you already know to get interviews or referrals. And you can make cold contacts to employers whose names you get from the *Yellow Pages* in the phone book.

This chapter shows you some very effective ways to use the telephone to find job openings and set up interviews.

Copyright © 1995 • JIST Works, Inc. • Indianapolis, IN 46202 • (317) 264-3720

Overcoming Phone Phobia

You may find it hard to use the phone in the way I suggest. Many people do. They think it is "pushy" to call someone and ask for an interview. Before you decide this technique is not for you, think about why you are afraid. What is the worst thing that can happen to you?

Most calls take only a minute or so. And most employers don't mind talking to a person they might be interested in hiring.

Making these calls does require you to overcome some shyness, but they are really quite easy to do.

I suggest that you start by making calls to people you know — your warm contacts. Then call the people they refer you to. This network of people is often happy to help you. Even people you just picked from the *Yellow Pages* will usually treat you well. The experience of thousands of job seekers is that very few people will be rude to you. And you probably wouldn't want to work for that sort of person anyway.

Sample JIST Card Phone Contact

You have already done a lot of work on your JIST Card. It can be used as the basis for what you say in a phone call. Look at the following example to see how one person used his JIST Card to develop a phone call. As you read the card, imagine you are an employer who hires people with these skills. Would you be interested in interviewing this person?

"Hello, my name is John Kijek. I am interested in a position as an auto mechanic. I have over three years of experience, including one year in a full-time auto mechanic's training program. I am familiar with all hand tools and basic diagnostic equipment, and can handle common auto repair tasks, such as tune ups, brakes, exhaust systems, electrical and mechanical repairs. I also work quickly, often completing jobs correctly in less than the standard time. I have all the tools needed to start work immediately. I can work any shift and prefer full-time work. I am also honest, reliable, and good with people. When may I come in for an interview?"

Copyright © 1995 • JIST Works, Inc. • Indianapolis, IN 46202 • (317) 264-3720

How Do You React to This Phone Call?

Directions: *Before you go on, write how you might feel about a person who called you —an employer — with this approach. If you needed some-one like this, would you give him an interview?*

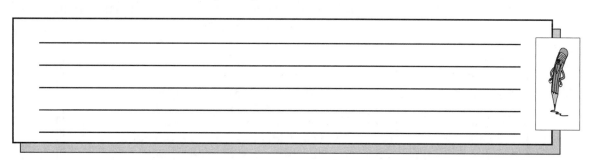

Just as with the JIST Card, most people say that this phone call gave them a positive impression. Most people also say they would give him an interview if they had an opening. Not everyone, but most. For this reason, reading a phone script based on your JIST Card is a very effective way to use the telephone.

Some General Tips for Completing Your Phone Script

To help you write your phone script, I've provided a worksheet later in this chapter. Read the tips carefully. Then use the information on your JIST Card to help you fill in each section of your Telephone Contact Worksheet. Write with a pencil or erasable pen so that you can rewrite or make changes easily.

Write Exactly What You Will Say on the Phone

A written script will help you present yourself effectively and keep you from stumbling around for the right word.

Keep Your Telephone Script Short

Just present the information an employer would want to know about you and ask for an interview. A good phone script can be read out loud in about 30 seconds or less. This is about the same time it takes to read a JIST Card. Short!

Write Your Script the Way You Talk

Since you have already completed your JIST Card, use it as the basis for your telephone script. Your JIST Card uses short sentences and phrases, and you probably wouldn't talk that way. So add some words to your script to make it sound natural when you say say it out loud.

Copyright © 1995 • JIST Works, Inc. • Indianapolis, IN 46202 • (317) 264-3720

Anatomy of a Phone Script

Here is another sample phone script. This one is a bit longer than the other sample but still can be read in about 30 seconds.

Just like a JIST Card, your phone script can be separated into separate sections. Each of the five parts of a phone script is pointed out in the sample below.

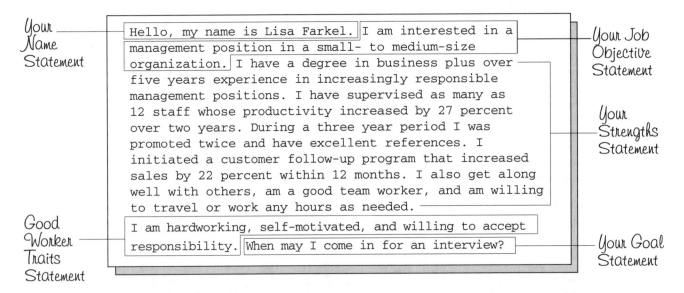

Your Name Statement

Hello, my name is Lisa Farkel. I am interested in a management position in a small- to medium-size organization. I have a degree in business plus over five years experience in increasingly responsible management positions. I have supervised as many as 12 staff whose productivity increased by 27 percent over two years. During a three year period I was promoted twice and have excellent references. I initiated a customer follow-up program that increased sales by 22 percent within 12 months. I also get along well with others, am a good team worker, and am willing to travel or work any hours as needed. I am hardworking, self-motivated, and willing to accept responsibility. When may I come in for an interview?

Your Job Objective Statement

Your Strengths Statement

Good Worker Traits Statement

Your Goal Statement

The Telephone Contact Worksheet

Directions: *Tips for writing each of the five parts of a phone script are provided in this worksheet. Read the tips for each part, them complete that section of the worksheet. Later, you can write your final version on another worksheet provided in this chapter.*

Your Name

This one is easy. All you have to do is fill in the blank.

Your name statement

Hello, my name is _____

Your Job Objective

Always begin your statement with "I am interested in a position as. . . ." After many years of experience, I know that this approach works! For example, if you were to say "Do you have any jobs?" the person you are calling can say "No." And that is not the response you want.

Copyright © 1995 • JIST Works, Inc. • Indianapolis, IN 46202 • (317) 264-3720

It takes you only about 30 seconds to read your phone script, and you don't want to get rejected before you begin. So don't use the word job in your first sentence. If you say you are "looking for a job", or anything similar, you often will be interrupted. Then you will be told there are no openings.

 If the job objective from your JIST Card sounds good when you say it out loud, just write it below and you are done. If it doesn't, change it around a bit until it does. For example, if your JIST Card says you want a "Clerical/General Office" position, your phone script might say this:

"I am interested in a clerical or general office position."

Your Job Objective Statement

I am interested in a position as _____

_____

_____

Your Strengths

The skills section of your JIST Card lists length of experience, training and education, special skills related to the job, and accomplishments. Your phone script will use much of the same content you used in these sections of your JIST Card.

 Rewriting the content from this part of your JIST Card may take some time. The sentences in your phone script must sound natural when spoken. You may find it helpful to write and edit this section on a separate piece of paper before writing it on the worksheet.

Your Strengths Statement

_____

_____

_____

_____

_____

_____

_____

_____

_____

_____

Your Good Worker Skills

Simply take the last line from your JIST Card and make these key adaptive skills into a sentence. For example, "Reliable, Hard Working, Learn Quickly" from a JIST Card might be written in a phone script as "I am reliable, hard working, and I learn quickly."

Your Good Worker Skills Statement

_____

_____

_____

Your Goal

Your goal is to get an interview. The closing statement has been filled in for you because — that's right — it works! If you said, for example, "May I come in for an interview?" the employer could say "No." And you don't want to make it easy for them to say no! Once again, after many years of experience, this is how I suggest you handle your final statement on your phone script.

Your Goal Statement

When may I come in for an interview?

The Final Phone Script

When practicing making a phone contact, it is important to have your written script in front of you. This will allow you to read it out loud until you know it from memory.

Directions: *Before you write your final script, you may want to read it out loud to one or more people. This will allow you to make any additional changes to it until it "sounds right." It may take several drafts on separate sheets of paper before you think it is in its final form. Once it is, write your final script on the next page. Write it out exactly as you will say it. Putting this all together in one place will make it easier to read later.*

Copyright © 1995 • JIST Works, Inc. • Indianapolis, IN 46202 • (317) 264-3720

NAME: *Hello, my name is* _____

POSITION: *I am interested in a position as* _____

_____

STRENGTHS: _____

_____

_____

_____

_____

_____

_____

_____

_____

_____

_____

_____

_____

_____

GOOD WORKER _____

TRAITS: _____

_____

_____

_____

GOAL: *When may I come in for an interview?* _____

Tips for Making Effective Phone Contacts

Now that you have developed your phone script, you need to know how to use it effectively. Here are more tried and true tips:

Get to the Hiring Authority

You need to get directly to the person who would supervise you. Unless you want to work in the Personnel Department, you wouldn't normally ask to talk to someone who does.

Depending on the type and size of the organization you're calling, you should have a pretty good idea of the title of the person who would supervise you. In a small business you might ask to speak to the "person in charge." In a larger one, you would ask for the name of the person who is in charge of a particular department.

Get the Name of a Person

If you don't have the name of the person you need to speak to, ask for it. For example, ask for the name of the person in charge of the accounting department if that is where you want to work. Usually, you will be given the supervisor's name and your call will be transferred to him or her immediately.

When you do get a name, get the correct spelling and write it down right away. Then you can use that person's name in your conversation.

Get Past the Receptionist

In some cases, receptionists and secretaries will try to screen out your call. If they find out you are looking for a job, they may transfer you to the Personnel Department or ask you to send an application or resume. Here are some things you can do to keep from getting screened out:

Call Back: Call back a day later and say you are getting ready to send some correspondence to the person who manages such and such. You want to use the correct name and title and request that they give you this information. This is true since you will be sending them something soon. And this approach usually gets you what you need. Say thank you and call back in a day or so. Then ask for the supervisor or manager by name.

Call When the Secretary Is Out: You are likely to get right through if you call when that receptionist is out to lunch. Other good times are just before and after normal work hours. Less experienced staff members are likely to answer the phones and put you right through. The boss also might be in early or working late.

When Referred by Someone Else

It is always best to be referred by someone else. If this is the case, immediately give the name of the person who suggested you call. For example, say:

"Hello, Ms. Beetle. Joan Bugsby suggested I give you a call."

If the receptionist asks why you are calling, say:

"A friend of Ms. Beetle's suggested I give her a call about a personal matter."

When a friend of the employer recommends that you call, you usually get right through. It's that simple.

When Calling Someone You Know

Sometimes using your telephone script just as it is written on your worksheet will not make sense.

For example, if you are calling someone you know, you would normally begin

Copyright © 1995 • JIST Works, Inc. • Indianapolis, IN 46202 • (317) 264-3720

with some friendly conversation before getting to the purpose of your call. Then, you could use your phone script by saying something like this:

"*The reason I called is to let you know I am looking for a job, and I thought you might be able to help. Let me tell you a few things about myself. I am looking for a position as. . .*" (continue with the rest of your phone script here).

There are many other situations where you will need to adapt your basic script. Use your own judgment on this. With practice, it becomes easier!

Your Goal Is to Get an Interview

The primary goal of a phone contact is to get an interview. To succeed, you must be ready to get past the first and even the second rejection.

Ask Three Times for an Interview
You must practice asking three times for the interview!
Here is an example:

1. You: When may I come in for an interview?
   Employer: *I don't have any positions open now.*

2. You: That's OK, I'd still like to come in to talk to you about the possibility of future openings.
   Employer: *I really don't plan on hiring within the next six months or so.*

3. You: Then I'd like to come in and learn more about what you do. I'm sure you know a lot about the industry, and I am looking for ideas on getting into it and moving up.

Although this approach does not always work, asking the third time works more often than most people would believe! It is important to learn how to do this, since overcoming initial rejections is a very important part of getting to "Yes."

Arrange a Time

If the person agrees to an interview, arrange a specific date and time. If you are not sure of the correct name or address, call back later and ask the receptionist.

Sometimes an Interview Does Not Make Sense

Sometimes you will decide not to ask for an interview. The person may not seem helpful or you may have caught him or her at a busy time. If so, you can take another approach:

Get a Referral: Ask for names of other people who might be able to help you. Find out how to contact them. Then add these new contacts to your job search network!

Ask to Call Back: If your contact is busy when you call, ask if you can call back. Get a specific time and day to do this, and add the call to your to-do list for that day. If you do call back, the employer will be impressed. And she may give you an interview for just that reason.

Ask to Call Back from Time to Time: Ask if you can keep in touch. Maybe the employer will hear of an opening or have some other information for you. Many job seekers get their best leads from a person they have checked back with several times.

Follow Up!

It is important to follow up with each person you contact in your search for a job. This includes following up with people in your network, including those you phone. This effort can make a big difference in their remembering and helping you. Here are the best ways to follow up:

Send thank-you notes!

It is good manners to thank the person who helped you. Send a thank-you note right after the phone call. If you arranged for an interview, send a note saying you look forward to your meeting. If the contact gave you a referral to someone else, send another note telling her how things turned out. Or send a thank-you note telling her you followed up on her suggestion. Enclosing a JIST Card or resume is often a good idea, too.

Overcoming Fear and Phone Phobia, Part 2

Making phone calls is work. It sets you up for some rejection and failures. But, as I suggested earlier, what is the worst thing that can happen? Think about it.

One way to look at the job search process is as a series of no's. You need to get a lot of them before you finally get to the yes. Like this:

no no no no no no no no no no no no no no no no no no no no no no no no
no no no no no no no no no no no no no no no no no no no no no no no no
no no no no no no no no no no no no no no no no no no no no no no no **YES**

So you could think in terms of your task as getting quickly through the no's so that you can get to the yes.

Making phone calls is like that. You are more likely to do it if you schedule to make your calls every day. It is easiest if you plan to make your calls at a certain time each day. You should also have a goal, so decide how many calls you will make per day. Most job seekers can make ten to twenty calls per hour. And they often get an interview with this many calls. Not bad for an hour's work!

Copyright © 1995 • JIST Works, Inc. • Indianapolis, IN 46202 • (317) 264-3720

10

The Seven Phases of an Interview—And How to Succeed in Each

What Employers Really Want to Know

Interviewing for a job is one of the hardest parts of the job search. You may be a bit nervous about it yourself. You may have had a bad interview experience, and you don't look forward to another. Most people end up getting rejected. And they don't like it.

But it doesn't have to be that way. In your case, you know what you want to do. And you have the skills, experience, and training to do it. All you have to do is convince the employer that you can do the job. This chapter and the next will show you how.

Employers use an interview to evaluate you. Will you be able to do the job? Will you be a good employee? If they don't believe you are qualified and willing to work hard, you won't get a job offer. If you do meet their expectations, you may get an offer — or a referral. So you need to know what to do and say in a job interview. You need to meet an employer's expectations.

You looked at employer expectations in chapter 1. Because they are so important, let's review them here.

Expectation #1: Do You Look Like the Right Person?

Appearance: First impressions do count!
- Personal appearance and grooming
- Manner and social skills
- Paperwork including resumes and JIST Cards

Expectation #2: Can You Be Counted On?

Dependability
- Comes in on time and does not abuse days off
- Can be trusted
- Gets things done on time
- Gets along well with others
- Is productive and hard working

Expectation #3: Can You Do the Job?

Skills, Experience, Training and Education
- Has enough work experience to do the job
- Has the needed education and training
- Interests and hobbies support the job objective
- Has additional appropriate life experiences
- Shows a record of achievements
- Presents the ability to do the job

In one way or another, interviewers must find out about all these things. At every point in the interview process, they are evaluating you — even when you might least expect it.

The following section breaks the interview into seven phases or sections. As you learn to handle each one, you will be better able to meet an employer's expectations. If you do, you will be much more likely to get a job offer!

Copyright © 1995 • JIST Works, Inc. • Indianapolis, IN 46202 • (317) 264-3720

The Seven Phases of an Interview

No two interviews are alike. But there are similarities. If you look closely at the interview process, you can see separate phases. Looking at each phase will help you learn how to handle interviews well.

The Seven Phases of an Interview
1. Before You Go to the Interview
2. Opening Moves
3. The Interview Itself
4. Closing the Interview
5. Following Up
6. Negotiating Salary and Benefits
7. Making a Final Decision

Every phase of the interview is important. The following sections show you why and give you tips for handling each phase.

Phase 1: Before You Go to the Interview

Before you even meet, the interviewer can form an impression of you.

How First Impressions Are Made

Write at least two ways that you could make a good or a bad first impression before you even get to the interview:

1. _____

2. _____

There are many ways an interviewer can make judgments about you before you meet. For example, you may have spoken to the interviewer or the secretary

Copyright © 1995 • JIST Works, Inc. • Indianapolis, IN 46202 • (317) 264-3720

on the phone. You may have sent a resume or other correspondence. Or someone may have told her about you.

Before you meet an interviewer, here are some things to consider:

Appearance

You may not consider what follows as appearance issues, but they are. So be careful in all your early contacts with an employer. Do everything possible to create a good impression.

Dress and Grooming

How you dress and groom for an interview varies from job to job. You will have to make your own decisions about what is right for the jobs that interest you.

> ### Rule for Interview Dress and Grooming:
>
> **Dress (and groom) like the interviewer is likely to be dressed — but cleaner.**

You may not dress just like your supervisor, but looking like the boss is usually a good idea. Of course, different jobs and organizations require different styles of dress. For example, a person looking for a job as an auto mechanic would dress differently than one looking for an office job.

Because there are so many differences, there are no firm rules on how to dress. But there are things to avoid. Here are some important tips that will make sense in most situations:

- **Don't wear jeans, tank tops, shorts, or other very casual clothes:**
  Some clothing, even if it looks good on you, just isn't good for a serious interview. If you are in doubt about anything you're thinking of wearing, don't wear it.

- **Be conservative:**
  An interview is not a good time to be trendy. Traditional styles are particularly important for office jobs and in large, formal organizations.

- **Check your shoes:**
  One study found that employers reacted to the condition and style of a job seeker's shoes! Unshined shoes were an indication, they felt, of someone who was sloppy and would not work hard. Little things do count, so pay attention to everything you wear.

Copyright © 1995 • JIST Works, Inc. • Indianapolis, IN 46202 • (317) 264-3720

- **Colognes, aftershaves, make-up, jewelry:**

  Again, be conservative. Keep your makeup simple and avoid too much of anything. Use perfumes or colognes lightly or not at all.

- **Careful grooming is a must:**

  Get those hands and nails extra clean and manicured. Eliminate stray facial hairs. Get a simple hair style.

- **Spend some money if necessary:**

  Get one well-fitting "interview outfit." Get your hair styled. Look a bit sharper than you usually do. If you have a limited budget, borrow something that looks good on you! It's that important.

- **Consider using a "uniform":**

  Some styles are almost always acceptable in certain jobs. For men working in an office, a conservative business suit, white shirt, and conservative tie are always acceptable. A less formal approach would include gray slacks, a blue blazer, white or blue shirt, and a conservative tie. For women, there are many more alternatives, but a simple tailored skirt, matching jacket, and white blouse are a safe choice. Women should not wear informal clothing to a job interview.

- **Dress up, not down:**

  In jobs that don't require formal dress, plan to dress a few notches above the clothing you might normally wear in that job. You can, of course, overdress for an interview too. That's why my Rule for Interview Dress and Grooming is so important.

- **Ask for advice:**

  If you are not sure how to dress and groom for an interview, discuss proper interview dress and grooming with friends *(who have a good sense of style)* and family *(if you dare)* before you finally decide for yourself. You also can get good books at the library that give helpful tips for "dressing for success." And the staff at many full-service clothing stores may be able to give you advice.

After you've thought about it, write how you plan to dress and groom for an interview in the spaces below.

My Interview Outfit

_____

_____

_____

_____

_____

Research Before You Go

Know as much as you can about the organization before you go to an important interview. You should try to find out about the following things:

The Organization:

✔ Size, number of employees
✔ Major products or services
✔ Competitors and the competitive environment
✔ Major changes in policies or status
✔ Reputation, values
✔ Major weaknesses or opportunities

The Interviewer:

✔ Level and area of responsibility
✔ Special work-related projects, interests, and accomplishments
✔ Personal information (family, hobbies, etc.)
✔ What sort of boss he or she is
✔ Management style

The Position:

✔ Does an opening exist now or do similar jobs exist?
✔ What happened to others in similar positions?
✔ Salary range and benefits
✔ Duties and responsibilities
✔ What the last person did wrong *(so you can avoid it)* or right (so you can emphasize it)

Get There Early

Get to the interview a few minutes early. Make sure you know how to get there, and allow plenty of time to get there. If necessary, call the receptionist for directions.

Final Grooming

Before you go in for the interview stop in a rest room. Look at yourself in a mirror and make any final adjustments.

Waiting Room Behavior

Assume that interviewers will hear about everything you do in the waiting room. They will ask the receptionist how you conducted yourself — and how you treated the receptionist.

 Copyright © 1995 • JIST Works, Inc. • Indianapolis, IN 46202 • (317) 264-3720

The Receptionist

The receptionist's opinion of you matters. So go out of your way to be polite and friendly. If you spoke to the receptionist on the phone, mention that and express appreciation for any help you were offered.

If the Interviewer Is Late

If the interviewer is late, you are lucky. He or she will probably feel bad about keeping you waiting and may give you better-than-average treatment to make up for it.

If you have to wait more than 20 minutes or so, ask to reschedule your appointment at another time. You don't want to act as if you have nothing to do. And, again, the interviewer will probably make it up to you later.

Some Self-Improvement Notes

Consider what you have learned about Phase 1 of an interview and note any specific ideas to improve your interview performance.

_____

_____

_____

_____

_____

Phase 2: Opening Moves

The first few minutes of an interview are very important. If you make a bad impression, you probably won't be able to change it.

Once Again, First Impressions Count

You already know how important your dress and grooming are. What else do interviewers react to? List here at least three things interviewers can observe as they first meet you that would affect their impression of you.

1. _____

2. _____

3. _____

Copyright © 1995 • JIST Works, Inc. • Indianapolis, IN 46202 • (317) 264-3720

Interviewers react to many things you say and do during the first few minutes of an interview. Here are some of the things they mention most often:

Initial Greeting

Be ready for a friendly greeting! Show you are happy to be there. Although this is a business meeting, your social skills will be considered, too. A firm, but not crushing, handshake is needed unless the interviewer does not offer to shake hands. Use her last name in your greeting if possible, as in "It's good to meet you Ms. Kelly." And make sure you get her name and status technically and politically correct! This might require you to call in advance to make sure.

Posture

How you stand and sit can make a difference. You look more interested if you lean forward in your chair when talking or listening. If you lean back, you may look too relaxed.

Voice

You may be nervous, but try to sound enthusiastic and friendly. Your voice should be neither too soft nor too loud. Practice sounding confident.

Eye Contact

People who don't look at a speaker's eyes are considered shy, insecure, and even dishonest. Although you should never stare, you look more confident when you look at the interviewer's eyes while you listen or speak. Don't stare, of course.

Distracting Habits

You may have nervous habits you don't even notice. But pay attention! Most interviewers find such habits annoying. For example, do you:

✔ Play with your hair or clothing?
✔ Say something like "You know?" or "Uhh" over and over?
 (*"Uhh, you know what I mean?"*)

The best way to see yourself as others do is to have someone videotape you while you role-play an interview. If that is not possible, become aware of how others see you, and then try to change your negative behavior. Your friends and relatives also can help you notice annoying habits you have that could bother an interviewer.

Establishing the Relationship

Almost all interviews begin with informal chitchat. Favorite subjects are the weather, whether you had any trouble getting there, and similar topics. This informal talk seems to have nothing to do with the interview; but it does. These first

Copyright © 1995 • JIST Works, Inc. • Indianapolis, IN 46202 • (317) 264-3720

few minutes allow an interviewer to relax you and find out how well you relate to others socially.

There are many things you could do during the first few minutes of an interview. The following are some suggestions from experienced interviewers.

- Allow things to happen.
  Relax. Don't feel you have to start a serious interview right away. Go with the chitchat, if that is what the employer wants to do.

- Smile.
  Look and sound happy to be there and to meet the interviewer.

- Use the interviewer's name.
  Be formal. Use "Mister Rogers" or "Ms. Evans" unless you are asked to use another name. Use his or her name as often as you can in your conversation.

- Compliment something in the interviewer's office.
  Look for something you can compliment or something you have in common. Most offices have photographs or other things you can comment on. Say how great her kids look or ask whether he decorated the office himself.

- Ask some opening questions.
  After a few minutes of friendly talk, you could ask a question to get things started. For example:
  "I'd like to know more about what your organization does. Would you mind telling me?"
  or
  "I have a background in _____ and I'm interested in how these skills might best be used in an organization such as yours."

Some Self-Improvement Notes

Consider what you have learned about Phase 2 of an interview and note any specific ideas to improve your interview performance.

Phase 3: The Interview Itself

This is the most complicated part of the interview. It can last from 15 to 45 minutes or more while the interviewer tries to find your strengths and weaknesses.

Interviewers may ask you almost anything. They are looking for any problems you may have. They also want to be convinced that you have the skills, experience, and personality to do a good job.

If you have made a good impression during the earlier phases on an interview, you can use this phase to talk about your qualifications.

Answering Problem Questions

In one survey, employers said that more than 90 percent of the people they interviewed for a job could not answer a problem question. More than 80 percent could not explain the skills they had for the job. Obviously, this is a serious problem for most job seekers. Lack of comunication skills will keep many of them from getting a good job that will require their other skills.

Ten Tough Questions

The following list shows the ten problem questions you are most likely to be asked during your interview. They may not be asked in just this way, but the interviewer **is** looking for answers to these questions.

The Ten Most Frequently Asked Interview Questions

1. Why don't you tell me about yourself?
2. Why should I hire you?
3. What are your major strengths?
4. What are your major weaknesses?
5. What sort of pay do you expect to receive?
6. How does your previous experience relate to the jobs we have here?
7. What are your plans for the future?
8. What will your former employers (or references) say about you?
9. Why are you looking for this sort of position and why here?
10. Why don't you tell me about your personal situation?

Copyright © 1995 • JIST Works, Inc. • Indianapolis, IN 46202 • (317) 264-3720

The next chapter shows you how to answer these questions. It also shows you how to answer other difficult interview questions. For now, let's look at the remaining phases of an interview.

Some Self-Improvement Notes

 Consider what you have learned about Phase 3 of an interview and note any specific ideas to improve your interview performance.

_____

_____

_____

_____

_____

_____

Phase 4: Closing the Interview

All good things must end. You can close an interview as effectively as you began it. While this part of an interview is often overlooked, it can make a big difference.

Summarize at the End

As an interview is about to close, take a few minutes to summarize your key points. If any problems or weaknesses came up, state why they will not keep you from doing a good job.

Point out the strengths you have for this job and why you believe you can do it well.

Ask for the Job

If you are interested in the job, say so! If you want this job, ask for it! Many employers hire one person over another just because one person really wants it. And says so.

Use the Call-Back Close

The call-back close is a technique that can end the interview to your advantage. It will take some practice. You may not be comfortable with it at first. But it works! The next page shows how it works.

Copyright © 1995 • JIST Works, Inc. • Indianapolis, IN 46202 • (317) 264-3720

The Call-Back Close

1. Thank the interviewer by name.
2. Express interest in the job and organization.
3. Arrange a reason and a time to call back.
4. Say good-bye.

A Sample Call-Back Close

Here's an example of a call-back interview close:

Thank the interviewer by name:

While shaking hands, say "Thank you *(Mr. or Mrs. or Ms. Whomever)* for your time today."

Express interest:

Tell the employer that you are interested in the position or organization *(or both!)*, whichever makes sense. For example, *"The position we discussed today is just what I have been looking for. And I am very impressed by your organization, too."*

Arrange a reason and a time to call back:

If the interviewer has been helpful, he or she won't mind your following up. It's important that you arrange a day and time to call. Never expect the employer to call you. Say something like this, *"I'm sure I'll have questions. When would be the best time for me to get back to you?"*

Say good-bye:

After you've set a time and date to call back, thank the interviewer by name and say good-bye. Like this, *"Thank you, Mr. Mullahy, for the time you gave me today. I will call you next Tuesday morning, between 9 and 10 o'clock."*

Some Self-Improvement Notes

Consider what you have learned about Phase 4 of an interview and note any specific ideas to improve your interview performance.

_____

_____

_____

_____

_____

Copyright © 1995 • JIST Works, Inc. • Indianapolis, IN 46202 • (317) 264-3720

Phase 5: Following Up

Once you've left the interview it's over. Right? Not really. You need to follow up! This can make the difference between your getting the job and someone else getting it. Here are some things you must do.

Send a Thank-You Note

As soon as possible after the interview — and no later than 24 hours — send a thank-you note. Enclose a JIST Card, too.

Make Notes

Write yourself notes about the interview while it is still fresh in your mind. You will not remember details in a week or so.

Follow Up As Promised

If you said you would call back next Tuesday at 9 o'clock, do it. You will surely impress the interviewer with how well organized you are.

Thank-You Notes

Sending a thank-you note is a simple act of appreciation that hardly anyone ever does. Thank-you notes show your appreciation. And they also have practical benefits, too. People who receive them will remember you. But employers say they rarely get thank-you notes. They describe people who do send them with positive terms, such as thoughtful, well organized, and thorough.

A thank-you note won't get you a job you're not qualified for, but it will impress people. When a job opens up, they will remember you. People in your job search network will also be more interested in helping you. If they know of an opening or meet someone who does, they will think of you.

Some Tips for Writing Thank-You Notes

Here are some tips for preparing thank-you notes:

Paper and envelope	Use good quality note paper with matching envelopes. Most stationery stores have them. Avoid cute covers. A simple "Thank You" on the front will do. Off-white and buff colors look good.
Typed vs. handwritten	Handwritten notes are fine unless your handwriting is illegible or sloppy. If so, type them or have them done on a word processor.
Salutation	Unless you are thanking a friend or relative, don't use first names. Write *"Dear Ms. Krenshaw,"* rather than *"Dear Vera."* Include the date.
The note itself	Keep it short and friendly. This is not the place to write, *"The*

reason you should hire me is. . . ." Remember, the note is a thank-you for what the person did to help you. It is not a hard-sell pitch for what you want to get from them. As appropriate, be specific about when you will next contact them. If you plan to meet with the person soon, still send a note saying you are looking forward to the meeting and name the date and time.

Your signature
Use your first and last names. Avoid initials and make your signature legible.

When to send it
Send your note no later than 24 hours after you make contact. Ideally, you should write it immediately after the contact while the details are fresh in your mind. Always send a note after an interview, even if things did not go well. Its possible that the interviewer will feel badly too — and give you another chance.

Enclosure
Depending on the situation, a JIST Card is often the ideal enclosure for a thank-you note. It's a soft sell and provides your phone number if the person should wish to reach you. *("Gosh, that job just opened up! Who was that person who called me last week?")* Make sure your note cards are at least as big as the JIST Card so you don't have to fold the card.

Some Sample Thank-You Notes

2234 Riverwood Ave.
Philadelphia, PA 17963
April 16, 19XX

Ms. Helen A. Colcord
Henderson & Associates, Inc.
1801 Washington Blvd., Suite 1201
Philadelphia, PA 17963

Dear Ms. Colcord:

Thank you for sharing your time with me so generously today. I really appreciated seeing your state-of-the-art computer equipment.

Your advice has already proved helpful. I have an appointment to meet with Mr. Robert Hopper on Friday. As you anticipated, he does intend to add more computer operators in the next few months.

In case you think of someone else who might need a person like me, I'm enclosing another JIST Card. I will let you know how the interview with Mr. Hopper goes.

Sincerely,

William Richardson

William Richardson

Kay Howell
apartment 3C
1030 College Avenue
Denver, Colorado 80260

October 22, 1996

Mr. Robert A. Hernandez
Manager, Data Processing Division
Harmon Enterprises
4648 Pearl Street
Denver, Colorado 80442

Dear Mr. Hernandez,

Thank you for meeting with me today. I'm impressed by the high standards your department maintains. The more I heard and saw — the more interested I became in working for your firm.

As we agreed, I will call you next Monday, October 28. In the meantime, I would be pleased to answer any additional questions you may have.

Sincerely,

Kay Howell

Copyright © 1995 • JIST Works, Inc. • Indianapolis, IN 46202 • (317) 264-3720

Some Self-Improvement Notes

Consider what you have learned about Phase 5 of an interview and note any specific ideas to improve your interview performance.

_____

_____

_____

_____

Phase 6: Negotiating Salary and Benefits

Pay attention now. This information could end up being worth much more to you than the price of this book.

Let's imagine that the job you are interviewing for sounds ideal for you. But you still have to answer some tough questions.

What Would You Say?

Suppose the interviewer asks you, "What do you expect to get paid for this position?" What would you say? Write it here:

_____

_____

_____

_____

Whatever you say, you will probably lose. Suppose the employer was willing to pay $18,000 per year *(or $7 per hour or whatever)*. If you say you will take $16,500, guess what you will be paid? That may have been the most expensive ten seconds in your life!

There are other ways you can lose, too. The employer may decide not to hire you at all. He or she may think they need a person who is worth $20,000 — which leaves you out. If you were clever, you may have asked for $19,000 and hoped you would get it. You could lose here, too. Many employers would assume you'll be unhappy with the salary they had in mind. Even if you would have been happy to have it.

Copyright © 1995 • JIST Works, Inc. • Indianapolis, IN 46202 • (317) 264-3720

Salary Negotiation Rule 1:

Never discuss salary until you are being offered the job.

And now you understand why.

You will learn more about negotiating salaries and other benefits in the next chapter. This is one of the problem questions that most job seekers have trouble answering. Lots of trouble.

Some Self-Improvement Notes

Consider what you have learned about Phase 6 of an interview and note any specific ideas to improve your interview performance.

_____

_____

_____

_____

_____

Phase 7: Making a Final Decision

The interview process is not completely over until you accept a job. This can sometimes be an easy decision to make. There are other times when deciding can be very hard.

The worksheet in this section shows you how to put the positives and negatives of a difficult decision down on paper. People who use this process tend to make better decisions. Some research shows they also tend to be happier with what they did, even when it did not work out. You can use this form to help you make any decision.

This example shows how one person used the form to consider a job offer. You can make your own worksheet on a blank sheet of paper. The final decision will always be yours to make, but this form can help you make a good decision.

Copyright © 1995 • JIST Works, Inc. • Indianapolis, IN 46202 • (317) 264-3720

Sample Decision-Making Worksheet

Option Considered: _Director of Sales, Farkel's Foods_

	Positives	**Negatives**
Tangible Things for Me	1. More Money. 2. Work I will like better. 3. An office of my own. 4. A chance to travel.	1. Lots of pressure & long hours. 2. Less job security. 3. My boss is known to have a bad temper.
Tangible Things for Others	1. Can move back to the country. 2. Can afford better clothes & more recreation for the family. 3. Can start a college fund for the kids	1. I'll be away from home more often. 2. Less private time. 3. More driving. 4. Will be taking work home more often.
Self Approval/ Disapproval	1. I get to set my own goals & time tables, at least to a point. 2. I'll have a chance to become better known in the field.	1. I may feel guilty about being on the road so much and away from the family. 2. Other people in the firm may resent my status.
Social Approval/ Disapproval	1. My friends & family will be impressed. 2. Professionally, this company is a leader.	1. I'll have to prove myself to some of our old sales reps & customers.

Some Self-Improvement Notes

Consider what you have learned about Phase 7 of an interview and note any specific ideas to improve your interview performance.

_____

_____

_____

_____

_____

Practice for Successful Interviews

You have now learned about the seven phases of an interview. I hope that this information helps you to understand this complex interaction. In the next chapter you will learn to answer problem interview questions. Knowing how to answer these questions will help you to get the job you want!

Copyright © 1995 • JIST Works, Inc. • Indianapolis, IN 46202 • (317) 264-3720

11

Answering Problem Questions

Don't Be Caught by Surprise

*I*n chapter 10, you learned that an interview has seven phases. The third phase is the interview itself. This is the most complicated part of the interview. And it can last from 15 to 45 minutes or more. This is when the interviewer tries to find out about your your strengths and weaknesses.

Interviewers may ask you almost anything. They are looking for any problems you may have. They also want to be convinced that you have the skills, experience, and personality to do a good job.

Answering Problem Questions

The biggest challenge most job seekers face in this phase of an interview is answering a problem question. For example, write an answer to the following question. Keep your interview response short and positive.

Copyright © 1995 • JIST Works, Inc. • Indianapolis, IN 46202 • (317) 264-3720

"What are your plans for the future?"

_____

_____

_____

_____

Are you satisfied with what you wrote? Would your answer make a good impression on an interviewer? Would your answer meet one or more of an employer's expectations?

If you are like most job seekers, you can learn to do better. In one survey, employers said that more than 90 percent of the people they interviewed could not answer a problem question. More than 80 percent could not describe the skills they had for the job. This is a serious problem for most job seekers. It keeps many of them from getting a good job that will require their skills.

The following list shows the ten questions you are most likely to be asked during an interview. This is the same list you saw in chapter 10. While the questions may not be asked in these exact words, the interviewer is looking for answers to these and similar questions.

The Ten Most Frequently Asked Interview Questions

1. Why don't you tell me about yourself?
2. Why should I hire you?
3. What are your major strengths?
4. What are your major weaknesses?
5. What sort of pay do you expect to receive?
6. How does your previous experience relate to the jobs we have here?
7. What are your plans for the future?
8. What will your former employers (or references) say about you?
9. Why are you looking for this sort of position and why here?
10. Why don't you tell me about your personal situation?

Copyright © 1995 • JIST Works, Inc. • Indianapolis, IN 46202 • (317) 264-3720

Besides these questions, there are hundreds of others you could be asked. You could learn to answer some of them here, but the interviewer may ask you different ones. So it is more important to learn a method for answering *any* question than to memorize answers to some. Let's take some time now to learn a method for all kinds of difficult questions.

A Method You Can Use to Answer Almost Any Interview Question

Look at the "Three Steps to Answering Problem Questions." This approach gives you a simple way of looking at each question you are asked in an interview. With practice, you can use the steps to answer most interview questions.

Three Steps to Answering Problem Questions

Step 1: Understand What Is Really Being Asked!

The question usually relates to Employer's Expectation #2 about your adaptive skills and personality.

Can we depend on you?
Are you easy to get along with?
Are you a good worker?
The question may also relate to Employer Expectation #3:
Do you have the experience and training to do the job if we hire you?

Step 1

Step 2: Answer the Question Briefly and in a Non-Damaging Way.

Acknowledge the facts.
But present them as advantages, not disadvantages.

Step 2

Copyright © 1995 • JIST Works, Inc. • Indianapolis, IN 46202 • (317) 264-3720

Step 3: Answer the Real Concern by Presenting Your Skills!

Base your answer on your key skills, as listed on your JIST Card.

Give examples to support your skills statements.

Notice how important it is to know what an employer expects. If you don't remember, review chapter 1. The three major employer's expectations are listed there.

Using the Three Steps to Answer a Problem Question

Let me give you an example. Here is one of the ten questions you are likely to be asked in an interview:

"What are your plans for the future?"

How would you answer this? Let's use the Three Steps to see how you could give an honest answer that meets the employer's expectations.

Step 1: Understand What Is Really Being Asked

What does the interviewer really want to know? Look at the boxes of the Three Steps to Answering Problem Questions, and decide what the employer is looking for with this question. Write what you think is really being asked.

_____

_____

_____

_____

_____

_____

In this case, the interviewer probably wants to know if you are going to remain on the job long enough. And he or she probably wants to know that you *want* this particular kind of job in this type of organization. Saying that you hope to sail around the world may be interesting, but it would not be a good response.

Copyright © 1995 • JIST Works, Inc. • Indianapolis, IN 46202 • (317) 264-3720

Step 2: Answer the Question Briefly and in a Non-Damaging Way

First, answer the actual question as it is asked. For example, you could say:

> *"There are many things I want to do over the next five years. One is to get settled into the career I have decided on and learn as much as I can."*

This is a brief answer to the question. It doesn't say much and it doesn't hurt you, but it allows you to begin answering the real question. And the real question is probably a form of Employer's Expectation #2, "Can I depend on you?"

Step 3: Answer the Real Concern by Presenting Your Skills

> *"I've had a number of jobs (or one, been unemployed, or other experiences . . .) and I have learned to value a good, stable position. My variety of experiences is an asset because I have learned so many things I can now apply to this position. I am looking for a position where I can get totally involved, work hard, and do well."*

Depending on your own situation, there are many other things you could say. This response emphasizes the job seeker's stability. But, as brief as it is, this answer meets the employer's expectations.

Review the answer to this question that you wrote earlier in this chapter. If you are like most job seekers, your response could be improved. Using the Three Steps to answer this particular question as it relates to you, rewrite your answer.

Good Answers to the Ten Most Frequently Asked Interview Questions

Now, let's look at some tips for answering the top ten interview questions. Your own responses will be different from the examples I've given here. But if you use the Three Steps to Answering Problem Questions, you can learn how to answer each of these questions effectively. Then you'll be ready to do better than 90 percent of the job seekers who are competing with you.

Question 1: Why don't you tell me about yourself?

The interviewer does not want to know your life history! Instead, he or she wants you to tell how your background relates to doing the job. Following is a sample response.

> *"I grew up in the Southwest and my parents and one sister still live there. I always did well in school, and by the time I graduated from high school, knew I wanted to work in a business setting. I had taken typing and other business classes and had done well in them. And the jobs I've had while going to school have taught me how many small businesses are run. In one of these jobs, I was given complete responsibility for the night operations of a wholesale grocery business that grossed over two million dollars a year. I learned there how to supervise others and solve problems under pressure."*

This answer gives a very brief personal history and then gets right into the skills and experiences this of this job seeker. A different job would require you to stress different skills. Your personal history is also different, but you can still use the three basic steps to answering the question for yourself.

How would you answer this question in an interview? Use the three-step process to write your own answer below.

Your Answer to Problem Question #1:

_____
_____
_____
_____
_____
_____
_____
_____

Question 2: Why should I hire you?

This is the most important question of all! If you don't have a good reason, why "should" anyone hire you? It is not often asked this clearly, but this is "the" question behind many interview questions.

The best answer is to show how you can solve a problem for them, help the business make more money, or provide something else of value that they need. Think about the most valuable thing you can do for an organization. That is probably what you should include in your answer.

> Here is an example from a person with recent training but little work experience:
> *"I have over two years of training in this field and know about all the latest equipment and methods. That means I can get right to work and be productive almost right away. I am also willing to work hard to learn new things. During the entire time I went to school, I held a full-time job to help earn the tuition and support myself. I learned to work hard and concentrate on what was important. I expect to do the same thing here. Since I won't be going to school now, I plan on putting in extra time after regular work hours to learn anything this job needs."*

Copyright © 1995 • JIST Works, Inc. • Indianapolis, IN 46202 • (317) 264-3720

Now think about the job you want. What strengths can you bring to that job? Write your answer to the question below.

Your Answer to Problem Question #2:

_____

_____

_____

_____

_____

_____

_____

_____

Question 3: What are your major strengths?

This is a direct question with little hidden meaning. Answer it by emphasizing the adaptive skills you defined in chapter 3. These are the skills employers are most concerned about (Employer's Expectation #2). Here is one answer from a person who had little prior work experience:

> *"I think one of them is that you can depend on me. I work very hard to meet deadlines and don't need a lot of supervision in doing it. If I don't know what to do, I don't mind asking either. In high school I got a solid B-plus average even though I was very involved in sports. I always got my assignments in on time and somehow found the time to do extra credit work, too."*

Review chapter 3 and use at least two of your top adaptive skills in answering this question.

Your Answer to Problem Question #3:

_____

_____

_____

_____

_____

_____

_____

_____

Question 4: What are your major weaknesses?

This is a question most job seekers don't handle well. If you tell what you do poorly, you may not get the job. If you say you have no weaknesses, the interviewer won't believe you. Ask yourself what the interviewer really wants to know. They want to know that you are aware of your weaknesses. And that you have learned to overcome them so that they don't affect your work.

Using the three-step process, the second step would result in a response like this:

> *"I do have some weaknesses. For example, in previous jobs I would get annoyed with co-workers who didn't work as hard as I did. I sometimes said so to them and several times refused to do their work when they asked me to."*

But the response should not end there. The third step would result in a statement like this:

> *"But I have learned to deal with this better. I still work hard, but now I let the supervisor deal with another worker's problems. And I've also gained some skills as a supervisor myself. I've learned to motivate others to do more because they want to, not because I want them to."*

Did you notice that this weakness isn't such a weakness at all? Many of our strengths began in failure. We learned from them and got better.

 List some weaknesses of this type that you could use in your own answer. Now, pick one of these and use it to answer the question. Use the three steps!

Your Answer to Problem Question #4:

_____

_____

_____

_____

_____

_____

_____

Question 5: What sort of pay do you expect to receive?

Knowing how to answer this question could be worth a lot of money to you! In chapter 10 you learned that one of the interview phases is negotiating salary. This question deals with the the same issue. In that chapter, you learned this important rule in salary negotiation:

Copyright © 1995 • JIST Works, Inc. • Indianapolis, IN 46202 • (317) 264-3720

Salary Negotiation Rule 1:

Never discuss salary until you are being offered the job.

It might be helpful to review why this is so before you continue. Here are a few paragraphs from that chapter to refresh your memory:

Whatever you say, you will probably lose. Suppose the employer was willing to pay $18,000 per year (or $7 per hour or whatever). If you say you will take $16,500, guess what you will be paid? That may have been the most expensive ten seconds in your life!

There are other ways you can lose, too. The employer may decide not to hire you at all. He or she may think they need a person who is worth $20,000 — which leaves you out. If you were clever, you may have asked for $19,000 and hoped you would get it. You could lose here, too. Many employers would assume you'll be unhappy with the salary they had in mind. Even if you would have been happy to have it.

Good advice. But you didn't really learn how to answer the salary question. For this question, you need to remember the following three rules:

Salary Negotiation Rule 2:

Know the probable salary range in advance.

Before the interview, you need to know what similar jobs in similar types of organizations pay. This will give you an idea of what the position is likely to pay. To find out, ask others in similar jobs. The library is a good source of salary information. Ask the research librarian. You also can call your local state Employment Service's statistical office. They are required to keep this information for each area.

Copyright © 1995 • JIST Works, Inc. • Indianapolis, IN 46202 • (317) 264-3720

Salary Negotiation Rule 3:

Bracket your salary range.

If you think the employer pays between $18,000 and $22,000 per year, state your own range as "high teens to mid-twenties." That covers the amount the employer probably had in mind and gives you room to get more. Bracketing will not get you screened out, and it leaves open the possibility of getting more than your minimum.

Look over the examples below. The principles apply for any salary range, so simply translate the concept and apply it to the salary range that makes sense for you.

Some Examples of Salary Brackets

If They Pay:	You Say:
$7/hour	6 to 8 dollars per hour
$15,000/year	mid- to upper teens
$18,000/year	upper teens to low twenties
$22,000/year	low to mid-twenties
$27,500/year	upper twenties to low thirties
$90,000/year	high five figure to low six figure

OK, that last entry was for fun. But I hope you get the idea. Bracketing keeps your options open. It won't get you screened out and it may allow you to get a higher offer than you might have otherwise. Which brings us to my next rule:

Salary Negotiation Rule 4:

Never say no to a job offer before it is made or until 24 hours have passed.

Remember, the objective of an interview is to get a job offer. Many job seekers get screened out early in the interview by discussing salary. If you give the impression that the job doesn't pay what you had hoped, or that it paid more, you could get screened out. The best approach is to avoid discussing salary until you are

Copyright © 1995 • JIST Works, Inc. • Indianapolis, IN 46202 • (317) 264-3720

being offered the job. If the money is not what you had in mind, say you want to consider the offer and will call back the next day. You can always turn it down then.

You may also say that if the salary were higher you would take the position. Perhaps you could be given more responsibility to justify a higher wage? Or you could negotiate an increase after a certain period of time.

Do not negotiate like this unless you are willing to give up the offer. But you just might be able to get a counter-offer that you would accept.

 Now, go ahead and answer the question and use the bracking technique.

Your Answer to Problem Question #5:

_____

_____

_____

_____

_____

_____

_____

Question 6: How does your previous experience relate to the jobs we have here?

This one requires a direct response. This question is asking, "Can you prove you have the experience and skills to do the job?" It is directly related to Employer's Expectation #3. In some cases, other people with better credentials than yours will want the job you're after. You can even mention this, then explain why you are a better choice.

Here is an example of how one person handled this situation:

> *"As you know, I have over five years of experience in a variety of jobs. While this job is in a different industry, it will also require my skills in managing people and meeting the public. In fact, my daily contact with large numbers of people on previous jobs has taught me how to work under pressure. I feel very able to deal with pressure and to get the job done."*

One of the jobs this person had was as a waitress. She had to learn to handle people under pressure in such a job. By presenting the *skills* she used, her answer tells us she could use the same skills in other jobs.

Copyright © 1995 • JIST Works, Inc. • Indianapolis, IN 46202 • (317) 264-3720

Be sure to mention any specific skills or training you have that will help you do the job. Include your greatest job-related strengths in your own answer to this question:

Your Answer to Problem Question #6:

_____

_____

_____

_____

_____

Question 7: What are your plans for the future?

As you may recall, we covered this question earlier in this chapter. The interviewer is really asking whether you are likely to remain on the job. But an employer has many concerns, depending on your situation.

Some Concerns an Employer Has:

- Will you be happy with the salary? *(If not, you may leave.)*
- Will you leave to raise a family or relocate because of a spouse's job transfer?
- Do you have a history of leaving jobs after a short stay? *(If so, it seems likely you will do this again.)*
- Are you overqualified? *(and likely to be unhappy in this job — and eventually leave?)*

Depending on the situation, there may be other concerns, too. You may wish to practice answering this question again. If so, put yourself in an employer's place. Then answer the real question. Try to bring up anything in your own life situation that some employers might be concerned about. *And then write a response to the question that will put them at ease about you. (Of course, whatever you say should be true...)*

Your Answer to Problem Question #7:

_____

_____

_____

_____

_____

Copyright © 1995 • JIST Works, Inc. • Indianapolis, IN 46202 • (317) 264-3720

Question 8: What will your former employers (or references) say about you?

This question again goes after Employer's Expectation #2. The interviewer really wants to know about your adaptive skills and whether you can be depended on, and the other basics. Are you easy to get along with? Are you reliable?

Many employers will check your references. So if you are less than honest about problems in previous jobs, you could get caught! If everyone you ever worked for thinks you are great, answering this question will be easy. But almost everyone has had some type of a problem. If the interviewer is likely to find out about your problem by checking with previous employers, honesty could be the best policy. Consider telling it like it was and accept responsibility for being part of the problem.

Many employers have been fired sometime in their careers. It's no sin and often has little to do with being a good worker. If you learned something from the experience, say so.

In a way, this question is similar to asking you for your major weakness. A good answer can help you get the job — even if you have to reveal some negative information.

> "If you check with my two previous employers, they will both tell you that I am a good worker and that I do things right. But you may find out that one of them is not too enthusiastic about me. I really can't explain why we did not get along. I tried to do my best, but she passed me over for merit raises twice.
>
> She will tell you that I got the work done, but she may also tell you that I was not willing to socialize with the other workers after hours. I had a new baby and I was working full time. I was very reliable, but it was true that I didn't go out two or three times a week with the others. I felt uncomfortable there and eventually left on my own. My next job was with a boss who will say wonderful things about me. But I thought you might want to know."

It is always better to know in advance what a previous employer will say about you. If you do expect a problem from a previous employer, try to find out exactly what will be said. If possible, talk it over so you know exactly what he or she will say when giving a reference. Sometimes, you can get your employer to agree to avoid being negative. Ask him to write you a letter of reference. Usually he will not be too negative in a letter and your new employer may accept the letter and not call.

If you still know that this employer will give you a negative reference, think of someone else you worked with closely in the same organization. Ask that person to give you a reference instead.

Some organizations do not allow their supervisors to give out information on previous employees. They are afraid of being sued. So they only give out your dates of employment there and nothing else. Since a new employer can't find out about you, he or she may not take a chance. This situation makes it even more important for you to get letters of reference from those employers, if they are positive.

 Go ahead and answer the question now. Try to handle any problems you may have had with previous employers that will be found if references are checked.

Your Answer to Problem Question #8:

Question 9: Why are you looking for this sort of position and why here?

Employers know that you will do better in the job you really want. Employers want to make sure you know what you want. They also want you to tell them what you like about the job. And what you like about doing this job in their organization. The closer you come to wanting what they have, the better.

The best answer for this is the absolute truth. You should have a clear idea of the type of job you want before the interview. And you should know the sort of organization and people you want to work with. You gathered all of this information earlier in this book. If you are interviewing for a job you want, in a place where you think you would enjoy working, answering this question should be easy. You just need to tell the truth.

 Consider your reasons for wanting this type of job. Select your top two and include them in your answer. Since you don't yet have a particular employer to respond to, use your imagination to decide what the organization you're interviewing with is like. Then tell what you like about the organization and the job.

Your Answer to Problem Question #9:

Copyright © 1995 • JIST Works, Inc. • Indianapolis, IN 46202 • (317) 264-3720

Question 10: Why don't you tell me about your personal situation?

Very few interviewers will ask this question so directly. But they *do* want to know. They will often try to find out in casual conversation. While you may feel that this is none of their business, they may not hire you unless they feel comfortable about you and your personal situation.

If you follow the three-step process, you should first ask yourself what are they really asking? Their concern is about Employer's Expectation #2. The issue is whether you can be counted on. They will look for signs that you are unstable or unreliable.

There are now a variety of laws that restrict the types of questions an employer may directly ask without risk of a lawsuit. Even so, most employers do want to know enough about you to feel comfortable. They are, after all, people.

Following is a list of things related to your personal situation that an employer might wonder about. You could argue that interviewers would be unfair and biased if they asked some of these questions. But you must understand that they really only need to be told that you can be counted on. Even if you just moved here, even if you have kids, even if you are single.

Some Things an Employer Might Wonder About

The Question	An Employer's Real Concern
Are you single?	Will you stay?
Are you married?	Will you devote the time needed?
Do you have marital or family problems?	Missed work, poor performance or poor interpersonal skills?
How do you handle money or personal problems?	Theft, irresponsible?
Have you moved recently?	Will you move again?
How do you spend your free time?	Alchohol or substance abuse, other socially unacceptable behavior?
Do you have children?	Child care problems and days off?

Some Sample Responses to Question #10 (and Its Variations)

Following are some sample responses to direct or indirect questions about your personal situation. If one or more of these life situations are true for you, and they do not limit your ability to work, consider telling the interviewer. Even if he or she doesn't ask.

Copyright © 1995 • JIST Works, Inc. • Indianapolis, IN 46202 • (317) 264-3720

When responding to a question about your personal life, be friendly and positive. The message to give is that your personal situation will not hurt your ability to do a good job. Instead, suggest that your situation could offer some advantage to the organization! The responses that follow are all simple, direct, and positive. Each one also allows you to quickly move to presenting your skills.

Young children at home
"I have two children, both in school. Child care is no problem since they stay with a good friend."

Single head of household
"I'm not married and have two children at home. It is very, very important to me to have a steady income, and so child care is no problem."

Young and single
"I'm not married, and if I should marry, that would not change my plans for a full-time career. For now, I can devote my full attention to my career."

Just moved here
"I've decided to settle here in Depression Gulch permanently. I've rented an apartment, and the six moving vans are unloading there now."

Relatives, childhood
"I had a good childhood. Both of my parents still live within an hour's flight from here, and I see them several times a year."

Leisure
"For relaxation I grow worms in my spare time and am a member of the American Worm Growers Association."
(OK, that one may not be the best of responses, let's try another one...)
"My time is family-centered when I'm not working. I'm also active in several community organizations and spend at least some time each week in church activities."

All these responses could be expanded, but they should give you an idea of approaches you can take. And they all follow the principles presented in the Three Steps to Answering Problem Questions.

Other "Problem" Questions

Most people feel that employers will hold one particular thing against them. It may be something obvious, like age (being "too old" or "too young"). Or something not so obvious, like not having a degree. Or whatever. And most employers do hold one or another unfair bias.

But employers are also people. They generally try to be fair. And as employers, they are very interested in getting a good worker.

Your job is to make it easy for an interviewer to find out you *can* do the job. The problem is that many interviewers may *assume* you have a problem. They may not ask you directly if their assumption is true for you. And you won't have a chance to tell them that, in your case, their assumption is not true.

Copyright © 1995 • JIST Works, Inc. • Indianapolis, IN 46202 • (317) 264-3720

For example, if you are more than a little overweight, some employers may feel you will be often sick or be slow in your work. The interviewer will probably not bring it up. But this assumption can affect his opinion of you. Unless, somehow, you convince him that you are healthy, reliable, and quick.

You can bring up your weight or not. It is up to you. But it would be wise, if you do not bring it up directly, to emphasize that you do not fit any stereotype.

In almost all cases, the employer's assumptions have to do with, once again, Employer's Expectation #2. They need to know that they can depend on you to do the job. And if they don't ask, and you don't tell them, who will?

Here are sample statements covering typical "problems" that may concern an employer. Some are not fair or accurate assumptions. As a job seeker, though, you need to deal with what is real. Once you have the job, you can show them what is true for you.

Too Old

"I am a very stable worker requiring very little training. I have been dependable all my life, and I am at a point in my career where I don't plan on changing jobs. I still have ten years of work until I plan on retiring, which is probably longer than the average young person stays in a position these days." (Which is quite true, as most employers know.)

Too Young

"I don't have any bad work habits to break, so I can be quickly trained to do things the way you want. I plan on working hard to get established. I'll also work for less money than a more experienced worker. And I willl prove that I am worth more than I am paid."

Prison (or arrest) Record

"You need to know that I've spent time in jail. I learned my lesson and paid my debt to society for a mistake I have not repeated. While there, I studied hard and earned a certificate in this trade. I was in the top one-third of my class."

Physical Limitations

"Thank you for the job offer. Before I accept, you should know that I have a minor physical limitation, but it will not affect my performance on the job. . . ."

Unemployed

"I've been between jobs now for three months. During that time, I've carefully researched what I want to do and now I'm certain. Let me explain. . . ."

Overweight

"You may have noticed that I am a tad overweight. Some people think that overweight people are slow, won't work hard, or will be absent frequently. But let me tell you about myself. . . ."

Gender

"Not many women (or men) *are interested in these kinds of positions, so let me tell you why I am. . . ."*

Race

The best approach here is to assume there is no problem with your race. There usually is not and if there is, there shouldn't be. Present your skills, do your best, rest your case, send a thank-you note, and go on to set up the next interview. This advice is the same for all job-seekers.

National Origin

A lack of English language skills is a real limitation in getting many jobs and will often be a problem if you are limited in this way. If you are not a citizen of this country, employers will be concerned about your stability on the job — and they may be legally restricted in their ability to hire you. These are specialized problems where special help from the agencies who provide assistance to immigrants are best able to help. Even so, many employers will consider hiring you if you can present a good argument for doing so.

Physical Disability

Don't be defensive or clinical. If your disability is obvious, consider mentioning it in a matter-of-fact way. People will want to know that your disability will not be a problem, so explain why it won't be. Then emphasize why you can do the job better than the next job-seeker.

Illegal Questions

Some people argue that some of the questions in the previous section are illegal to ask. Some of the questions, if they were asked as presented, *would* be in poor taste. But this is a free country. Anyone can ask anything they want. It is what an interviewer *does* with the information that can be a problem. Hiring or not hiring people based on certain criteria is illegal.

There are a number of laws that protect people with certain characteristics from being kept out of jobs for those reasons alone. These laws require that a person be considered on the ability to do the job and no other criteria.

For example, a woman should be considerd fairly for a job as a carpenter based on her ability to do the job, not her gender. A person in a wheelchair should be fairly considered for a job as an accountant based on his or her accounting skills alone. A manager should be hired on his or her management skills and credentials, with race, religion or ethnic background not being an issue.

This is our right, to be treated fairly. And there is no question in my mind that this should be so.

As a job seeker, what's more important is whether or not you want the job. You don't have to answer any question if you don't want to. It's a free country for you, too. But you should understand by now that most questions are intended to find out if you will be a good employee. So why not say that, yes, there are good reasons that employers can count on you to do a good job.

If you don't like the interviewer or the way he or she asked a question, you can always say so. Or, if the interviewer is a jerk, you can get up and walk out of his or her office and go file a complaint with the authorities.

Fortunately, most employers are just like you are. They will be sensitive to your feelings and will treat you as an adult. They want to find someone that they belive will do a good job. There is a lot at stake for them, too, in making a hiring decision. So, ultimately, it is your responsibility to convince them you will be a good employee. Do not leave their impressions to chance. Tell them why they should hire you!

Copyright © 1995 • JIST Works, Inc. • Indianapolis, IN 46202 • (317) 264-3720

50 More Questions

Here is a list of 50 interview questions. It came from a survey of 92 companies who interviewed college students for jobs after graduation. Most of the questions are those asked of any adult. Look for the questions you would have trouble answering. These are the ones you need to practice answering! In doing so, remember to use the three-step process...

A List of Questions Often Asked by Employers

1. In what school activities have you participated? Why? Which do you enjoy the most?
2. How do you spend your spare time? What are your hobbies?
3. Why do you think you might like to work for our company?
4. What jobs have you held? How were they obtained, and why did you leave?
5. What courses did you like best? Least? Why?
6. Why did you choose your particular field of work?
7. What percentage of your school expense did you earn? How?
8. What do you know about our company?
9. Do you feel that you have received good general training?
10. What qualifications do you have that make you feel that you will be successful in your field?
11. What are your ideas on salary?
12. If you were starting school all over again, what courses would you take?
13. Can you forget your education and start from scratch?
14. How much money do you hope to earn at age 25? 30? 40?
15. Why did you decide to go to the school you attended?
16. What was your rank in your graduating class in high school? Other schools?
17. Do you think that your extracurricular activities were worth the time you devoted to them? Why?
18. What personal characteristics are necessary for success in your chosen field?
19. Why do you think you would like this particular type of job?
20. Are you looking for a permanent or temporary job?
21. Are you primarily interested in making money or do you feel that service to your fellow human beings is a satisfactory accomplishment?
22. Do you prefer working with others or by yourself?
23. Can you take instructions without feeling upset?
24. Tell me a story!
25. What have you learned from some of the jobs you have held?
26. Can you get recommendations from previous employers?
27. What interests you about our product or service?
28. What was your record in the military service?
29. What do you know about opportunities in the field in which you are trained?
30. How long do you expect to work?
31. Have you ever had any difficulty getting along with fellow students and faculty? Fellow workers?
32. Which of your school years was most difficult?
33. Do you like routine work?
34. Do you like regular work?
35. What is your major weakness?
36. Define cooperation.
37. Will you fight to get ahead?
38. Do you have an analytical mind?
39. Are you willing to go where the company sends you?
40. What job in our company would you choose if you were entirely free to do so?
41. Have you plans for further education?
42. What jobs have you enjoyed the most? The least? Why?
43. What are your own special abilities?
44. What job in our company do you want to work toward?
45. Would you prefer a large or a small company? Why?
46. How do you feel about overtime work?
47. What kind of work interests you?
48. Do you think that grades should be considered by employers?
49. Are you interested in research?
50. What have you done that shows initiative and willingness to work?

Plus One More Question

What is the one question you are most afraid an employer will ask? Write it here. Then use the three-step process to give a positive answer that an employer could accept.

The question: _____

_____

The answer: _____

_____

_____

_____

_____

_____

_____

There you have it. You are now better prepared for a job interview than most other job seekers. If you do well, you will be considered for jobs over people with better credentials. The more interviews you have, the better you will get. And you will get job offers.

Copyright © 1995 • JIST Works, Inc. • Indianapolis, IN 46202 • (317) 264-3720

12

How to Write Resumes and Cover Letters

And Use Them to Get Interviews!

Many resume books and job search "experts" tell you that a good resume is important. They say that a well-done resume will help you get an interview over others whose resumes are not as good.

While it is true that a poorly done resume can get you screened out, a resume alone is not a good tool for getting an interview. The best way to get an interview is through direct contact with people. As you learned in earlier chapters, most people find their jobs through one of two techniques. They get leads from people they know *(warm contacts)* or by making direct contacts with employers *(cold contacts)*.

Copyright © 1995 • JIST Works, Inc. • Indianapolis, IN 46202 • (317) 264-3720

Why Even a "Great" Resume Won't Get You a Job

Sending out lots of resumes is not an effective way to get a job. While almost any technique does work for some people, the odds are not in your favor. When used this way, the resume just delays your making direct contact with a potential employer. It also puts your resume onto a pile of other resumes from people who are competing for the same job. Even with a good resume, you are far more likely to get screened out in this situation.

Resume experts who tell you to make a great resume and then send it out to lots of people are giving old-fashioned advice. They assume that the way to get a job is to deal with personnel offices, go after publicly advertised jobs, and use passive job search methods. Instead, this book teaches you to use techniques that are effective with large as well as smaller employers *(that may not have a personnel office),* to go after the hidden job market of jobs that are not advertised *(where about 75 percent of all jobs are found)* and to use active techniques.

You Need a Resume Because . . .

While a resume is not a good tool to get you an interview, there are still some reasons for you to have one.

Why You Need a Resume
1. Employers expect you to have one.
2. A good resume will help you present what you have to offer an employer.

Employers use resumes to find out about your credentials and experience. Covering these details in an interview is not the best use of that valuable time. A well-written resume also forces you to summarize the highlights of your experience. When you've done this, you are better able to talk about yourself during the interview.

While many books continue to tell job seekers to send out lots of resumes in hopes of getting an interview, here is better advice.

Copyright © 1995 • JIST Works, Inc. • Indianapolis, IN 46202 • (317) 264-3720

The Five Most Effective Ways to Use a Resume

> ## The Five Most Effective Ways to Use a Resume
> 1. Get the interview first.
> 2. Send your resume.
> 3. Follow up with a JIST Card and thank-you note.
> 4. Send your resume and JIST Card to everyone in your growing job search network.
> 5. Send your resume in the traditional way, if you can't make direct contact.

Some Details on the Five Most Effective Ways to Use Your Resume

Even if you have written an excellent resume, it won't get you interviews unless you use it effectively. Following are some details on how to best use your resume to get more interviews.

1. **Get the interview first.** It is almost always better to first contact the employer by phone or in person before you send a resume. If possible, get a referral from someone you know. Or make a cold contact. In either case, ask for an interview. If no opening is available now, ask to come in and discuss the possibility of future openings.

2. **Send your resume.** Send your resume *after* you schedule an interview, so the employer can read about you before your meeting. Then valuable interview time can be spent discussing your skills rather than details that are best presented in a resume.

3. **Follow up with a JIST Card and thank-you note.** Immediately after each and every interview, send a thank-you note — and enclose one of your JIST Cards.

4. **Send your resume and JIST Card to everyone in your growing job search network.** This is an excellent way for people in your network to help you find unadvertised job leads. They can pass them along to others who might be interested in a person with your skills.

5. **Send your resume in the traditional way if you can't make direct contact.** An example would be answering a want ad with only a box number for an address. Just don't expect much to happen.

Copyright © 1995 • JIST Works, Inc. • Indianapolis, IN 46202 • (317) 264-3720

Some Tips on Writing an Effective Resume

There are no firm rules for writing a good resume. Every resume can be different. But here are some tips that I have learned are important in writing any resume.

Write It Yourself

Look at the sample resumes in this book *(and in other sources)*, but don't use their content in your own resume. If you do, your resume will sound like someone else. Many employers will know you didn't write it yourself — and that will not help you.

Make Every Word Count

Most resumes should be limited to one page — or two at the most. After you have written a first draft, edit it at least two more times. If a word or phrase does not support your ability to do the job, cut it out. Short is often better.

Make It Error Free

Just one error on your resume can create a negative impression. That could be enough to get you screened out. So ask someone else to check your resume for grammar and spelling errors. Check each word again before you have your resume printed. You just can't be too careful.

Make It Look Good

Have your resume professionally done and reproduced on good quality paper. Appearance, as you know, makes a lasting impression.

Stress Your Accomplishments

A resume is no place to be humble. Emphasize what you got done, and the results.

Be Specific

Give facts and numbers to support your accomplishments. Instead of saying you are good with people, say "I supervised and trained five staff and increased their productivity by 30 percent." The sample resumes and JIST Cards included in this book often include numbers. They do make a difference.

Copyright © 1995 • JIST Works, Inc. • Indianapolis, IN 46202 • (317) 264-3720

Don't Delay

Don't delay your job seach while working on a "better" resume! Many job seekers say they are still improving their resume when they should be out looking for a job. A better approach is to do a simple, error-free resume at first. Then actively look for a job. You can always work on a better version at night and on weekends.

Keep It Lively

Keep it short. Use action verbs and short sentences. Keep it interesting.

The Three Basic Types of Resumes

Resume styles vary. The two most common types are the *chronological* and *skills* resumes. This chapter shows you how to develop both of these types and shows you samples of each. There are also samples of a third resume type, the *combination* resume. This resume combines parts of both the chronological and the skills resumes.

Each of these resume styles has advantages and disadvantages. The best type of resume for you to use will depend on your situation. Let's look at each type of resume and learn more about their advantages for different situations.

The Chronological Resume

"Chronology" refers to time. A *chronological* resume begins with your most recent work or other experiences and moves back in time.

Look at the sample chronological resume that follows. Notice the job objective and how the job seeker's experience is organized.

While this resume could be improved, it does present the facts and would be an acceptable resume for many employers.

Copyright © 1995 • JIST Works, Inc. • Indianapolis, IN 46202 • (317) 264-3720

A Basic Chronological Resume Example

Judith J. Jones

115 South Hawthorne Avenue
Chicago, Illinois 46204
(317) 653-9217 (home)
(317) 272-7608 (message)

JOB OBJECTIVE

Desire a position in the office management, secretarial, or clerical area. Prefer a position requiring responsibility and a variety of tasks.

EDUCATION AND TRAINING

Acme Business College, Indianapolis, Indiana
Graduate of a one-year business/secretarial program, 1995

John Adams High School, South Bend, Indiana
Diploma: Business Education

U.S. Army

Financial procedures, accounting functions. Other: Continuing education classes and workshops in Business Communication, Scheduling Systems, and Customer Relations.

EXPERIENCE

1995-1995 — Returned to school to complete and update my business skills. Learned word processing and other new office techniques.

1992-1995 — Claims Processor, Blue Spear Insurance Co., Indianapolis, Indiana. Handled customer medical claims, used a CRT, filed, miscellaneous clerical duties.

1990-1992 — Sales Clerk, Judy's Boutique, Indianapolis, Indiana. Responsible for counter sales, display design, and selected tasks.

1988-1990 — Specialist, U.S. Army. Assigned to various stations as a specialist in finance operations. Promoted prior to honorable discharge.

Previous Jobs — Held part-time and summer jobs throughout high school.

PERSONAL

I am reliable, hardworking, and good with people.

Copyright © 1995 • JIST Works, Inc. • Indianapolis, IN 46202 • (317) 264-3720

An Improved Chronological Resume Example

This resume is for the same person, but adds details and makes other improvements on the previous example.

Judith J. Jones

115 South Hawthorne Avenue
Chicago, Illinois 46204
(317) 653-9217 (home)
(317) 272-7608 (message)

JOB OBJECTIVE

Seeking position requiring excellent management and secretarial skills in office environment. Position should require a variety of tasks including typing, word processing, accounting/bookkeeping functions, and customer contact.

EDUCATION AND TRAINING

Acme Business College, Indianapolis, Indiana.
Completed one-year program in Professional Secretarial and Office Management. Grades in top 30 percent of my class. Courses: word processing, accounting theory and systems, time management, basic supervision, and others.

John Adams High School, South Bend, Indiana.
Graduated with emphasis on business and secretarial courses. Won shorthand contest.

Other: Continuing education at my own expense (Business Communications, Customer Relations, Computer Applications, other courses).

EXPERIENCE

1995-1995 — Returned to business school to update skills. Advanced course work in accounting and office management. Learned to operate word processing and PC-based accounting and spreadsheet software. Gained operating knowledge of computers.

1992-1995 — Claims Processor, Blue Spear Insurance Company, Indianapolis, Indiana. Handled 50 complex medical insurance claims per day — 18 percent above department average. Received two merit raises for performance.

1990-1992 — Assistant Manager, Judy's Boutique, Indianapolis, Indiana. Managed sales, financial records, inventory, purchasing, correspondence, and related tasks during owner's absence. Supervised four employees. Sales increased 15 percent during my tenure.

1988-1990 — Finance Specialist (E4), U.S. Army. Responsible for the systematic processing of 500 invoices per day from commercial vendors. Trained and supervised eight employees. Devised internal system allowing 15 percent increase in invoices processed with a decrease in personnel.

1984-1988 — Various part-time and summer jobs through high school. Learned to deal with customers, meet deadlines, work hard, and other skills.

SPECIAL SKILLS AND ABILITIES

Type 80 words per minute and can operate most office equipment. Good communication and math skills. Accept supervision, able to supervise others. Excellent attendance record.

Copyright © 1995 • JIST Works, Inc. • Indianapolis, IN 46202 • (317) 264-3720

Advantages and Disadvantages of a Chronological Resume

This resume format has both advantages and disadvantages.

Advantages:

One big advantage is that this is the simplest and quickest resume style to write. Many employers want to know details about where you have worked in the past, including dates employed. This is a good resume style to use if you have a good work history in jobs similar to those you want now.

Disadvantages:

A chronological resume may display your weaknesses. It will quickly show an employer things like gaps in employment, frequent job changes, lack of work experience related to your job objective, recent graduation, and other potential problems. If you have one or more of these situations, a traditional chronological resume may not be best for you.

A Humble Suggestion

A chronological resume is simple and quick to do. For this reason, I suggest you complete a simple chronological resume before making a "better" one. You might even be able to get a job offer before you finish your improved version . . .

The Skills Resume

The skills resume is sometimes called a *functional* resume. In this format, your experience is organized under key skills. A well-done skills resume emphasizes skills that your job objective requires. These should also be the same skills that you are good at and want to use.

Look at the resume that follows and notice how it emphasizes skills rather than employment dates and job titles. It is an example of a simple skills resume.

Copyright © 1995 • JIST Works, Inc. • Indianapolis, IN 46202 • (317) 264-3720

A Skills Resume Example

ANDREA ATWOOD

3231 East Harbor Road
Grand Rapids, Michigan 41103

Home: (303) 447-2111   Message: (303) 547-8201

Objective: A responsible position in retail sales.

Areas of Accomplishment:

Customer Service	● Communicate well with all age groups.
	● Able to interpret customer concerns to help them find the items they want.
	● Received 6 Employee of the Month awards in 3 years.
Merchandise Display	● Developed display skills via in-house training and experience.
	● Received Outstanding Trainee award for Christmas Toy Display
	● Dress mannequins, arrange table displays, and organize sale merchandise.
Stock Control and Marking	● Maintained and marked stock during department manager's 6-week illness.
	● Developed more efficient record-keeping procedures.
Additional Skills	● Operate cash register and computerized accounting systems.
	● Willing to work evenings and weekends.
	● Punctual, honest, reliable, and hard-working.

Experience: Harper's Department Store
Grand Rapids, Michigan
Two years total experience

Education: Central High School
Grand Rapids, Michigan
3.6/4.0 grade point average
Honor Graduate in Distributive Education

Two years retail sales training in Distributive Education. Also courses in Business Writing, Computerized Accounting, and Word Processing.

Copyright © 1995 • JIST Works, Inc. • Indianapolis, IN 46202 • (317) 264-3720

Advantages and Disadvantages of a Skills Resume

As with a chronological resume, the skills resume has both good and not-so-good points.

Advantages:

A skills resume allows you to present accomplishments from all your life experiences. It is a good format when you need to "hide" problems that a chronological resume might show. For example, Andrea's resume does a good job of presenting what she can do, without making it obvious that her work experience was limited to part-time and summer jobs. Nor does it say that she is a recent graduate.

A well-written skills resume presents your strengths and avoids showing your weaknesses. For example, it can hide limited paid work experience, gaps in your job history, and little or no paid work experience in the field you want to get into now.

Disadvantages:

Because a skills resume can hide details that can be used to screen people out, some employers don't like them. Skills resumes can also be much harder to write than a chronological resume.

The Combination Resume

A combination resume includes elements of both the chronological and skills formats. I have included several samples of this type of resume at the end of this chapter. Look them over for ideas to use in your own resume.

This is a good type of resume to use if you have a reasonably good work history, but want the advantages that a skills resume has. For example, you may want to emphasize certain skills you have or include other life experiences besides work to support your skills.

Whatever type of resume you choose, there are many things you can do to make it stand out. You can use the following tips in writing any resume. As you look over the sample resumes in this chapter for ideas on doing your own, notice how they handle each of these issues.

Copyright © 1995 • JIST Works, Inc. • Indianapolis, IN 46202 • (317) 264-3720

Your Name

Use your formal name instead of a nickname.

Address

Avoid abbreviations and include your zip code. If you might move, use a relative's address or arrange with the post office to forward your mail to your new address.

Telephone Number

It's important for employers to be able to reach you, even if they can only leave messages. If your home phone is not always answered during the day, give a second number. Or use an answering machine. Include your area code.

Job Objective

Include your job objective in all but the most basic resume. Look at the examples to see how others have handled this. Notice that Judith didn't narrow down her options by saying "secretary" *(a job title)* or "clerical" *(entry-level jobs)*.

Education and Training

List any job-related training or education, including military. A recent graduate should emphasize special skills and accomplishments that directly relate to doing the job. If your education and training are important parts of your credentials, put them at the top. However, people with five or more years of work experience usually place this information at the end of their resumes.

Previous Experience

List your most recent job first, then work your way back. Show promotions as separate jobs. Cluster jobs held long ago or not related to your present objective. These could include the part-time jobs you had while going to school.

If you have little work experience, list unpaid work *(such as helping with the family business)* and volunteer jobs in place of paid jobs. Always emphasize the skills you used in these experiences that will help you in the job you want now. There is no need to mention that this work was unpaid.

Job Gaps

Your list of work experience may have gaps. You may have been going to school, having a child, working for yourself, or had other reasons for not working. Present this time positively. "Self-employed" or "Returned to school to improve my business skills" is better than saying "unemployed."

You can avoid showing you did not have a job at certain times by listing years or seasons. For example, if you didn't work from late January to early March you can write just your years of employment and not the months. For example:

Copyright © 1995 • JIST Works, Inc. • Indianapolis, IN 46202 • (317) 264-3720

Job A: 1995-1996   Job B: 1996-1998

No one can tell there was a two-month space between jobs.

Job Titles

Many people have more responsibilities than their job titles suggest. Some titles are unusual and won't mean much to most people. In these cases, use a title that more accurately tells what you did. For example, say "Shift Manager" rather than "Waiter" if you were actually in charge of things. Of course, make sure that you don't misrepresent your responsibilities.

Accomplishments

An employer wants to know what work you did well and other experiences. Just as in an interview, list some of your best accomplishments. Emphasize the number of people you served, units produced, staff trained, sales increased, and any other measurable achievements. You should also include special activities or accomplishments from other life activities such as your time in school.

Personal Data

This information is definitely optional. Who cares how tall you are? Or that you like to read romance novels? Some information can be put in this section, but only if it supports the job objective.

References

Don't list references on your resume. If employers want them, they will ask. Even saying, "References available on request" at the end of your resume adds nothing. If you have particularly good references, you can say something like, "Excellent references from previous employers are available." This sentence can be in the personal section.

And a Few Words on Honesty

A good resume presents your strengths and not your weaknesses. But this does not mean that you should misrepresent yourself. Do not claim you have skills you do not have, a degree you did not earn, or make any other claim that is not true. It just isn't the right thing to do. And, of course, many employers will fire you for doing this, should they find out. Which, of course, would serve you right.

Copyright © 1995 • JIST Works, Inc. • Indianapolis, IN 46202 • (317) 264-3720

Resume Design and Production Tips

Getting It "Typed" or Word Processed

Make sure your resume looks good. Using a computer word processor and laser printer will result in the best-looking resume. This is the way most resumes are now done, and I have included several sample resumes that were produced this way at the end of the chapter. A high quality typewriter also can produce an acceptable resume. Resumes produced on a computer dot-matrix printer or sloppy type from an old typewriter is not acceptable.

If You Don't Have a Computer or a Good Typewriter

If you are not experienced in using a computer word processor, now is not the time to learn. Trust me on this. Most small print shops and resume-writing services can produce a professional looking resume for a modest cost. Unless you need help in writing your resume, a one-page resume should cost no more than $50.

Of course, if you do have access to a good typewriter or computer system, this will allow you to customize your resume for specific employers.

Get Lots of Copies

In an earlier chapter, I showed you how you can develop hundreds of job leads through networking and by using cold contacts. It is to your advantage to give each and every one of these contacts one or more copies of your resume. So plan on having lots of copies available. You may go through several hundred before you land your next job.

Where and How to Get Copies

Few employers anymore expect an "original" typed copy of a resume. A good quality photocopy is acceptable for most situations. If you have access to a computer, laser printers provide excellent quality copies. Older "impact" or "daisey wheel" printers produce good quality originals similar to those produced on a typewriter.

If you don't have regular access to a computer system or good quality copy machine, you can get good photocopies made at most quick-print shops. These same shops can also print your resume on offset printing equipment if you are willing to buy several hundred at one time. Look in the *Yellow Pages* for listings.

Use Good Paper and Matching Envelopes

Most print shops will also have a supply of good quality papers and matching envelopes for use with resumes and cover letters. The best papers have a rich look and texture. They cost more, but are worth every penny. Ivory, white, and off-white are conservative colors that look professional.

Copyright © 1995 • JIST Works, Inc. • Indianapolis, IN 46202 • (317) 264-3720

A Few Final Words on Resumes

Even the best of resumes will not get you a job. You will have to do that yourself. And, to do so, you will have to get interviews and do well in them. Interviews are where the job search action is, not resumes.

Don't listen to resume experts. If you ask ten people for advice on your resume, they will all be willing to give it — yet no two of them will agree. You will have to make up your own mind about your resume. Feel free to break any "rules" if you have a good reason for doing so. It's your resume.

Don't avoid the job search by worrying about your resume. Write a simple and error-free resume, then go out and get lots of interviews. Later, you can write a better resume — if you want or need to.

Look over the sample resumes. I have included a variety of resumes at the end of this chapter. Some of them break rules and none of them is perfect. However, they are all based on real resumes written by real people *(though the names and other details have been changed)*. So look them over, then write your own.

How to Write Cover Letters

This type of letter was originally called a cover letter because it went along with, and "covered," a resume. Different situations need different types of letters. The sample cover letters in this section deal with a variety of typical situations. Look them over for ideas to use when writing your own letters.

You may find that you don't need to send many formal letters. Many job seekers get by with informal thank-you notes sent with copies of resumes and JIST Cards. But certain types of jobs, and some organizations, require a more formal approach. Use your judgment.

As always, make certain that all your job search correspondence makes a good impression. Sample cover letters are at the end of this chapter for you to review.

Some Tips for Writing and Using Superior Cover Letters

Here are some additional suggestions to help you create and use superior cover letters.

Send It to Someone By Name

Get the name of the person who is most likely to supervise you. Call first to get an interview. Then send your letter and resume.

Copyright © 1995 • JIST Works, Inc. • Indianapolis, IN 46202 • (317) 264-3720

Get It Right

Make sure you get the person's name, organization name, and address right. Include the person's correct job title. Make sure that your letter does not contain any grammar errors or other errors since this will create a poor impression.

Be Clear about What You Want

If you want an interview, ask for it. If you are interested in that organization, say so. Give clear reasons why they should consider you.

Be Friendly and Professional

A professional, informal style is usually best. Avoid a hard-sell "Hire me now!" approach. No one likes to be pushed.

Make It Look Good

Just as with a resume, any correspondence to an employer must look good. Use good quality paper and matching envelopes. A standard business format is good for most letters.

Target Your Letter

Typical reasons for sending a cover letter include: responding to an ad, preparing an employer for an interview *(the best reason!)*, and following up after a phone call or interview. Each of these letters will be different. Samples for each situation are included with the sample letters.

Follow Up

Remember that contacting an employer directly is much more effective than sending a letter. Don't expect letters to get you many interviews. They are best used to follow up *after* you have contacted the employer.

Sample Resumes

Comments: This resume uses a chronological format but adds an Additional Qualifications section to emphasize statements that did not fit into a traditional chronological format. Note that his unconventional approach to the Work Experience section allows him to emphasize skills and accomplishments.

Jack B. Harris

12 Browertown Road   Little Falls, NJ 07424   (201) 785-3011

Class A Automotive Mechanic
Specializing in complete engine overhaul and front end repair work

Education & Training

Graduate of Rockford Community College, 1989
Basic and Advanced Automotive Technology courses. GPA: 93
ASE Certified in repair of:

✓ Engines   ✓ Steering   ✓ Brakes
✓ Suspensions   ✓ Cooling systems   ✓ Electrical systems

GM training on the job:

✓ Use of infrared engine analyzers and other electronic test devices.
✓ Computerized diagnostics and service to electronic fuel injection, ignition, and emission control components.

Additional Qualifications

✓ Experience with foreign and domestic late model cars, vans and light trucks.
✓ Stay current on new technology; understand and act on instructions from repair manuals and manufacturers' bulletins.
✓ Very service oriented, hard working and cooperative.
✓ Own power hand tools for most common applications; able to do heavy lifting.

Work Experience

1991 - Present   **Master Automotive Technician**
                         DRISCOLL CHEVROLET/GEO, South Caldwell, NJ

✓ Attained highest status at dealership employing 12 technicians because of quick ability to diagnose troubles and make accurate repairs.
✓ Kept track of recurring problems in certain models for manufacturer notification. Shared information with other mechanics.
✓ Increased department profitability by consistently performing most services in 10-20% less time than alloted by industry standards.
✓ Contributed to 29% increase in customer satisfaction levels over the last 3 years.

1989 - 1991   **Automotive Mechanic**
                      SEARS AUTO CENTER, Clairmont, NJ

✓ Started with basic tune-ups and tire service, advancing after 2 months to brake, wheel alignment and radiator/air conditioning repairs.
✓ Was often assigned to customers with complaints of unsatisfactory original service. Corrected problems and maintained good relationships.
✓ Trained 4 newly hired mechanics in shop procedures.

(This resume example was submitted by Melanie A. Noonan, a professional resume writer in West Paterson, NJ.)

Comments: This one page chronological resume presents her limited work experience very effectively by emphasizing accomplishments. Notice the frequent use of numbers and percentages to support her accomplishments. While her resume does not say so, it is obvious that she works hard and puts lots of energy into her work and that she gets results.

Maria Marquez

4141 Beachway Road   (213) 449-2279
Redondo Beach, California 90277   (213) 540-3152

Objective: Management Position in a Major Hotel

Summary of Experience: Four years experience in sales, catering, banquet services, and guest relations in 300-room hotel. Doubled sales revenues from conferences and meetings. Increased dining room and bar revenues by 44%. Won prestigious national and local awards for increased productivity and services.

Experience: Park Regency Hotel, Los Angeles, California
Assistant Manager
1995 to Present

● Oversee a staff of 36, including dining room and bar, housekeeping, and public relations operations.

● Introduced new menus and increased dining room revenues by 44%. Gourmet America awarded us their Hotel Haute Cuisine first place award in both 1994 and 1995.

● Attracted 28% more diners with the first revival of Big Band Cocktail Dances in the Los Angeles area.

Kingsmont Hotel, Redondo Beach, California
Sales and Public Relations
1994 to 1995

● Doubled revenues per month from conferences and meetings.

● Redecorated meeting rooms and updated sound and visual media equipment. Trained staff to operate and maintain equipment.

● Instituted Outstanding Employee Courtesy awards, which resulted in an upgrade from B- to AAA+ in the Car and Travel Handbook.

Education: Associate Degree in Hotel Management from Henfield College of San Francisco. One year with the Boileau Culinary Institute, where I won the 1992 Grand Prize Scholarship. Bachelor of Arts in English Literature, University of Virginia.

Copyright © 1995 • JIST Works, Inc. • Indianapolis, IN 46202 • (317) 264-3720

Sample Resumes

Comments: Here is a two-page resume of a recent graduate who uses a combination format. He emphasizes his recent education and provides details of accomplishments and adaptive skills while there. The skills format used later in the resume allows him to present his recent schooling as real experience and to emphasize key transferable skills from previous jobs. Even his chronological listing of work experience emphasizes key adaptive and transferable skills needed in his current objective — even from jobs that don't seem at first to support his job objective.

Jonathan McLaughlin

673 Wickham Road
Phoenix, AZ 85009

(602) 253-9678 home
(602) 257-6643 messages

JOB OBJECTIVE

Position in the electronics industry requiring skills in the design, sale, installation, maintenance, and repair of audio, video, and other advanced electronics. Prefer tasks needing creative problem-solving skills and customer contact.

EDUCATION

PHOENIX TECHNICAL INSTITUTE
Phoenix, AZ
AS Degree,
Electronics Engineering
Technology
1994 - present

Completed a comprehensive, two-year curriculum including over 2,000 hours of class and advanced laboratory. Theoretical, practical, and hands-on knowledge of audio and RF amplifiers, AM/FM transmitter-receiver circuits, OP amplifiers, microwave and radar communications, digital circuits, and much more. Excellent attendance while working part time to pay tuition. Graduating in top 25% of class.

PLAINS JR. COLLEGE
Phoenix, AZ

Courses included Digital Electronics, Programming, business, and computer applications. Worked full time and maintained a B+ average.

DESERT VIEW HS
1992 graduate

College prep courses including advanced math, business, marketing, merchandising, computer orientation, and computer programming. Very active in varsity sports. National Jr. Honor Society for two years.

SKILLS

PROBLEM-SOLVING: Familiar with the underlying theory of most electronic systems and am particularly strong in isolating problems by using logic and persistence. I enjoy the challenge of solving complex problems and will work long hours, if necessary, to meet a deadline.

INTERPERSONAL: Have supervised five staff and trained many more. Comfortable with one-to-one and small group communications. Can explain technical issues simply to customers of varying levels of sophistication. Had over 10,000 customer contacts and several written commendations.

TECHNICAL: Background in a variety of technical areas including medical equipment, consumer electronics, computers, automated cash registers, photocopiers, and standard office and computer equipment and peripherals. Have designed special applications using sequential logic circuits and TTL logic. Constructed a microprocessor and wrote several machine language programs for this system. Can diagnose and repair problems in digital and analog circuits.

ORGANIZATIONAL: Have set up and run my own small business and worked in another responsible job while going to school full-time. Earned enough money to live independently and pay all school expenses during this time. I can work with minimal supervision and have learned to use my time efficiently.

EXPERIENCE

BANDLER'S INN: 1993 - present. Waiter, promoted to night manager. Complete responsibility for all operations of a shift grossing over $500,000 in sales per year. Supervised five full-time and three part-time staff. Business increased during my employment by 35% and profits by 42%, much of it due to word-of-mouth advertising of satisfied customers.

FRANKLIN HOSPITAL: 1992 - 1993. Electronic Service Technician Assistant. Worked in Medical, Physics, and Electronics Departments. Assisted technicians in routine service and maintenance of a variety of hospital equipment. Part-time while going to school.

TOM'S YARD SERVICE: 1991 - 1992. Set up a small business while in school. Worked part time and summers doing yard work. Made enough money to buy a car and save for tuition.

Sample Resumes

Comments: Here is a resume for someone with substantial work experience. He emphasizes skills related to his job objective in the first section of his resume and then includes his work history in chronological form later, including only details that support his current job objective. He also relates his military experience in an effective way. I've included his JIST Card here to show you how these two job search tools can relate to one another effectively.

Peter Neely

Messages: (237) 649-1234
Beeper: (237) 765-9876

Position: Truck Driver

Background and Skills: Over fifteen years of stable work history including no traffic citations or accidents. Formal training in diesel mechanics and electrical systems. Am familiar with most major destinations and have excellent map reading and problem solving abilities. I can handle responsibility and have a track record of getting things done.

Excellent heath, good work history, dependable

Peter Neely

203 Evergreen Road
Houston, Texas 39127
Messages:(237) 649-1234   Beeper:(237) 765-9876

POSITION DESIRED: Truck Driver

SKILLS

Summary of Work Experience: Over twenty years of stable work history, including substantial experience with diesel engines, electrical systems, and truck driving.

Driving Record/ Licenses: Chauffeur's license, qualified and able to drive anything that rolls. No traffic citations or accidents for over 20 years.

Vehicle Maintenance: I maintain correct maintenance schedules and avoid most breakdowns as a result. Substantial mechanical and electrical systems training and experience permits many breakdowns to be repaired immediately and avoid towing.

Record Keeping: Excellent attention to detail. Familiar with recording procedures and submit required records in on a timely basis.

Routing: Knowledge of many states. Good map reading and route planning skills.

Other: Not afraid of hard work, flexible, get along well with others, meet deadlines, responsible.

WORK EXPERIENCE

1995 - Present *CAPITAL TRUCK CENTER, Houston, Texas*
Pick up and deliver all types of commercial vehicles from across the United States. Am trusted with handling large sums of money and handling complex truck purchasing transactions.

1990 - 1995 *QUALITY PLATING CO., Houston, Texas*
Promoted from production to Quality Control. Developed numerous production improvements resulting in substantial cost savings.

1988 - 1990 *BLUE CROSS MANUFACTURING, Houston, Texas*
Received several increases in salary and responsibility before leaving for a more challenging position.

1984 - 1988 *Truck delivery of food products to destinations throughout the south.* Also responsible for up to 12 drivers and equipment maintenance personnel.

Prior to 1984 *Operated large diesel-powered electrical plants.* Responsible for monitoring and maintenance on a rigid schedule.

OTHER

Four years experience in the U.S. Air Force operating power plants. Stationed in Alaska, California, Wyoming, and other states. Honorable discharge. High school graduate plus training in diesel engines and electrical systems. Excellent health, love the outdoors, stable family life, non-smoker and no drinking.

Copyright © 1995 • JIST Works, Inc. • Indianapolis, IN 46202 • (317) 264-3720

Sample Resumes

Comments: Here is an example of a resume with a JIST Card done for the same person. Jane has lots of work experience and presents it effectively here. Note how well she uses this resume to emphasize things she did in previous jobs to support her current job objective. It also includes numbers to support her results.

Comments: Jane's JIST Card summarizes key skills and information that is presented in much greater detail in her resume. While JIST Cards are covered in another chapter, I thought that you would like to see how the resume/JIST Card combination can look.

Jane Craig

(412) 437-6217
Message: (412) 464-1273

Position PROGRAMMER/SYSTEMS
Desired: MANAGEMENT

Skills: Over 10 years combined education and experience in data processing, business and related fields. Programming ability in COBOL, RPG, BASIC and FORTRAN. Knowledge of various data base and applications programs in networked PC, Mac, and mainframe environments. Substantial business experience including accounting, management, sales and public relations.

Dedicated, self-starter, creative, dependable and willing to relocate.

Jane Craig

Career Objective	Challenging position in programming or related areas which would best utilize expertise in the business environment. This position should have many opportunities for an aggressive, dedicated individual with leadership abilities to advance.
Programming Skills	Includes functional program design relating to business issues including payroll, inventory and data base management, sales, marketing, accounting, and loan amortization reports. In conjunction with design would be coding, implementation, debugging, and file maintenance. Familiar with distributed network systems including PCs and Macs and working knowledge of DOS, Novel, UNIX, COBOL, Basic, RPG and FORTRAN. Also familiar with mainframe environments including tape and disk file access, organization and maintenance.
Areas of Expertise	Interpersonal communication strengths, public relations capabilities, innovative problem solving, and analytical talents.
Sales	A total of nine years experience in sales and sales management. Sold security products to distributors and burglar alarm dealers. Increased company's sales from $16,000 to over $70,000 per month. Creatively organized sales programs and marketing concepts. Trained sales personnel in prospecting techniques while also training service personnel in proper installation of alarms. Result: 90% of all new business was generated through referrals from existing customers.
Management	Managed burglar alarm company for four years while increasing profits yearly. Supervised office, sales, and installation personnel. Supervised and delegated work to assistants in accounting functions and inventory control. Worked as assistant credit manager, responsible for over $ million per month in sales. Handled semi-annual inventory of five branch stores totaling millions of dollars and supervised 120 people.
Accounting	Balanced all books and prepared tax forms for burglar alarm company. Eight years experience in credit and collections, with emphasis on collections. Collection rates were over 98% each year and was able to collect a bad debt deemed "uncollectible" by company in excess of $250,000.
Education	School of Computer Technology, Pittsburgh, PA Business Application Programming/TECH EXEC- 3.97 GPA Robert Morris College, Pittsburgh, PA Associate degree in Accounting, Minor in Management

2306 Cincinnati Street, Kingsford, PA 15171 (412) 437-6217
Message: (412) 464-1273

Copyright © 1995 • JIST Works, Inc. • Indianapolis, IN 46202 • (317) 264-3720

Sample Resumes

Comments: This two page resume is adapted from one presented in Richard Lathrop's book titled Who's Hiring Who, Ten Speed Press. Susan is a homemaker but note how a skills resume format allows her to present this experience so effectively.

SUSAN SMITH

1516 Sierra Way
Piedmont, California 97435
Telephone: (416) 486-3874

OBJECTIVE

Program Development, Coordination, and Administration

...especially in a people-oriented organization where there is a need to assure broad cooperative effort through the use of sound planning and strong administrative and persuasive skills to achieve community goals.

MAJOR AREAS OF EXPERIENCE AND ABILITY

Budgeting and Management For Sound Program Development

With partner, established new association devoted to maximum personal development and self-realization for each of its members. Over a period of time, administered budget totaling $485,000. Jointly planned growth of group and related expenditures, investments, programs, and development of holdings to realize current and long-term goals. As a result, holdings increased twenty-fold over the period, reserves invested increased 1200% and all major goals for members have been achieved or exceeded.

Purchasing to Assure Smooth Flow of Needed Supplies and Services

Made purchasing decisions to assure maximum production from available funds. Determined on-going inventory needs, selected suppliers, and maintained a strong continuing line of credit while minimizing financing costs. No significant project was ever adversely affected by lack of necessary supplies, equipment, or services on time.

Personnel Development and Motivation

Developed resources to assure maximum progress in achieving potential for development among all members of our group. Frequently engaged in intensive personnel counseling to achieve this. Sparked new community progress to help accomplish such results. Although arrangements with my partner gave me no say in selecting new members (I took them as they came), the results produced by this effort are a source of strong and continuing satisfaction to me. (See "Some Specific Results")

Susan Smith

Page Two

Transportation Management

Determined transportation needs of our group and, in consultation with members, assured specific transportation equipment acquisitions over a broad range of types (including seagoing). Contracted for additional transportation when necessary. Assured maximum utilization of limited motor pool to meet often-conflicting requirements demanding arrival of the same vehicle at widely divergent points at the same moment. Negotiated resolution of such conflicts in the best interest of all concerned. In addition, arranged four major moves of all facilities, furnishings, and equipment to new locations.

Other Functions Performed

Duties periodically require my action in the following additional functional areas: crisis management; proposal preparation; political analysis; nutrition; recreation planning and administration; stock market operations; taxes; building and grounds maintenance; community organization; social affairs administration (including VIP entertaining); catering; landscaping; (two awards for excellence); contract negotiations; teaching and more.

Some Specific Results

Above experience gained in 10 years devoted to family development and household management in partnership with my husband, Harvey Smith, who is equally responsible for results produced. Primary achievements: Daughter Sue, 12, leading candidate for the U.S. Junior Olympics team in gymnastics. A lovely home in Piedmont (social center for area teenagers). Secondary achievements: Vacation home at Newport, Oregon (on the beach) and a cabin in Big Sur. President of Piedmont High School PTA two years. Organized successful citizen protest to stop incursion of Oakland commercialism on Piedmont area.

PERSONAL DATA AND OTHER FACTS

Often complimented on appearance. Bachelor of Arts (Business Administration), Cody College, Cody, California. Highly active in community affairs. Have learned that there is a spark of genius in almost everyone which, when nurtured, can flare into dramatic achievement.

Copyright © 1995 • JIST Works, Inc. • Indianapolis, IN 46202 • (317) 264-3720

Sample Cover Letters

Sample Cover Letter: For a Specific Opening

Comments: This new graduate called first and arranged an interview — the best approach of all. She mentions specifically how she changed procedures for a business and saved money. Note how she includes skills such as "hard worker" and "deadline pressure," reviewed earlier in this book.

Wendy Presson
113 So. Meridian Street
Greenwich, Connecticut 11721
March 10, 19XX,

Ms. Willa Hines
New England Power and Light Company
604 Waterway Blvd.
Parien, Connecticut, 11716

I am following up on the brief chat we had today by phone. After getting the details on the position you have open. I am certain that it is the kind of job I have been looking for. A copy of my resume is enclosed providing more details of my background. I hope you have a chance to review it before we meet next week.

My special interest has long been in the large-volume order processing systems that your organization has developed so well. While in school I researched the flow of order processing work for a large corporation as part of a class assignment. With some simple and inexpensive procedural changes I recommended, check-processing time was reduced by an average of three days. For the number of checks and dollars involved, this one change resulted in an estimated increase in interest revenues of over $35,000 per year. Details do count!

While I have recently graduated from business school, I do have considerable experience for a person of my age. I have worked in a variety of jobs dealing with large numbers of people and deadline pressure. My studies have also been far more "hands-on" and practical than those of most schools, so I have a good working knowledge of current business systems and procedures. This includes a good understanding of various computer spreadsheet and applications programs, the use of automation, and experience with cutting costs and increasing profits. I am also a hard worker and realize I will need to apply myself to get established in my career.

I am most interested in the position you have available and am excited about the potential it offers. I look forward to seeing you next week.

Sincerely,

Wendy Presson

Wendy Presson

Sample Cover Letter: After an Interview

Comments: The writer uncovered a problem during an interview and afterward offers to solve the problem when no job exists. Many job seekers never think of scheduling an interview when there is no job opening, but many jobs are created this way to accommodate a good person.

Sandra A. Kijeh
115 So. Hawthorn Drive
Port Charlotte, Florida 81641

April 10, 19XX,

Christine Massey
Import Distributors., Inc.
417 East Main Street
Atlanta, Georgia 21649

Dear Ms. Massey,

I know you have a busy schedule so I was pleasantly surprised when you arranged a time for me to see you. While you don't have a position open now, your organization is just the sort of place I would like to work in. As we discussed, I like to be busy with a variety of duties and the active pace I saw at your company is what I seek.

Your ideas on increasing business sound creative enough to work. I've thought about the customer service problem and would like to discuss with you a possible solution. It would involve the use of a simple system of color-coded files that would prioritize older correspondence to give them a priority status. The handling of complaints could also be speeded up through the use of simple form letters similar to those you mentioned. I have some thoughts on how this might be done too, and will work out a draft of procedures and sample letters if you are interested. It can be done on the computers your staff already have and would not require any additional costs to implement.

Whether or not you have a position for me in the future, I appreciate the time you have given me. An extra copy of my resume is enclosed for your files or to pass on to someone else.

Let me know if you want to discuss the ideas I presented earlier in the letter. I will call you next week as you suggested to keep you informed of my progress.

Sincerely,

Sandra Kijeh

Sandra Kijeh

Sample Cover Letters

Sample Cover Letter: Following Up On a Cold Call

3321 East Haverford Road
Fort Howard Beach
North Carolina 49844

October 15, 19XX

Ms. Karen Miller
Office Manager Lendon, Lendon, and Sears
Suite 101, Landmark Building
Summit, NJ 11736

Dear Ms. Miller:

Enclosed is a copy of my resume which describes my work as a legal assistant. I hope this information will be helpful as a background for our interview next Monday at 4 o'clock.

I appreciated your taking time to describe your requirements so fully. This sounds like a position that could develop into a satisfying career. And my training in accounting, along with experience in using a variety of computer programs, seems to match your needs.

Lendon, Lendon, and Sears is a highly respected name in New Jersey. I am excited about this opportunity and I look forward to meeting with you.

Sincerely,

Richard Wittenberg

Richard Wittenberg

Sample Cover Letter: From a "Network" Contact

Comments: The person uses names from a professional association to conduct a long-distance job search. He explains the end of his old job, indicates certain skills, and mentins the availablity of positive references. He also requests an interview even though no job may be open.

John B. Goode
321 Smokie Way
Nashville, Tennessee 31201

July 10, 19XX

Paul Resley
Operations Manager
Rollem Trucking Co.
I-70 Freeway Drive
Kansas City, Missouri 78401

Mr. Resley,

I obtained your name from the membership directory of the Affiliated Trucking Association. I have been a member for over 10 years and I am very active in the Southeast Region. The reason I am writing is to ask for your help. The firm I had been employed with has been bought by a larger corporation. The operations here have been disbanded, leaving me unemployed.

While I like where I live, I know that finding a position at the level of responsibility I seek may require a move. As a center of the transportation business, your city is one of those I have targeted for special attention. A copy of my resume is enclosed for your use.

I'd like you to review it and consider where a person with my background would get a good reception in Kansas City. Perhaps you could think of a specific person for me to contact?

I have specialized in fast-growing organizations or ones that have experienced rapid change. My particular strength is in bringing things under control, then increasing profits. While my resume does not state this, I have excellent references from my former employer and would have stayed if a similar position existed at their new location.

As a member of the association, I hoped that you would provide some special attention to my request for assistance. Please call my answering service collect if you have any immediate leads. I plan on coming to Kansas City on a job-hunting trip within the next six weeks. Prior to then I will call you for advice on who I might contact for interviews. Even if they have no jobs open for me now, perhaps they will know of someone else who might!

Thanks in advance for your help on this.

Sincerely,

John B. Goode

John B. Goode
Treasurer, Southeast Region
Affiliated Trucking Association

Copyright © 1995 • JIST Works, Inc. • Indianapolis, IN 46202 • (317) 264-3720

13

Getting a Job Is a Job

Organizing Your Time

You now know more about finding a job than most people in North America. But the methods work only if you use them. This chapter will help you organize your time so that you get more interviews — and get a job in less time.

The More Interviews You Get, the Less Time It Takes to Get a Job

The average job seeker gets fewer than two interviews a month. At that rate, it takes an average of three to four months to find a job. Anything you can do to increase the number of interviews you get can decrease the time it takes to get a job. It's that simple.

Look at the chart that follows. It shows the number of interviews the average job seeker needs to get a job.

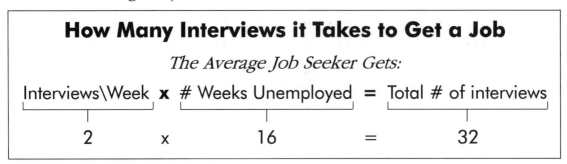

How Many Interviews it Takes to Get a Job		
The Average Job Seeker Gets:		
Interviews\Week **x**	# Weeks Unemployed =	Total # of interviews
2 x	16 =	32

And the More Time You Spend Looking, the More Interviews You Are Likely to Get

The average job seeker takes about sixteen weeks and thirty-two interviews to get a job. Many people who have used the techniques in this book get their jobs in much less time than the average.

Getting a job in less time does require you to work harder. Average job seekers only spend about fifteen hours a week actually looking for a job. That is one of the reasons they don't get more interviews.

This chapter will show you how to organize your time to get more interviews. It will show you how to turn your job search into a job itself. In a sense, getting a job is a job.

Set Up Your Job Search Office

To organize your job search as if it were a job, you need a place where you can work. Usually, this will be a place in your home set aside as your job search office. Following are some ideas to help you set up this office.

The Basics

A Telephone: A telephone is a basic tool for the job search. If you don't have one, ask to set up your office in the home of a friend or relative who has a phone.

Basic Furniture: You will need a table or desk to write on, a chair, and enough space to store your materials.

A Quiet Place: Just as on a job, you must have a place where you can concentrate. If you have children, arrange for someone else to care for them during your

Copyright © 1995 • JIST Works, Inc. • Indianapolis, IN 46202 • (317) 264-3720

"office" hours. Ask family or friends not to contact you at these hours. It is best to select a place where you can safely leave your materials. This will keep you from having them disturbed each day.

Materials You Will Need for Your Job Search Office

- Several good blue or black ink pen
- Pencils with erasers
- Lined paper for notes, contact lists, and other uses
- 3" x 5" cards for use as job lead cards
- 3" x 5" card file box with dividers
- Thank-you notes and envelopes
- Copies of resumes and JIST Cards
- Business-size envelopes
- Stamps
- *Yellow Pages* phone book
- Daily newspaper
- Calendars and planning schedules
- Career references and other books
- A copy of this book, of course

A good typewriter or computer word processor is also very helpful, if you can get one. Is there anything else you need? If so, continue your list here:

Set Up a Weekly Job Search Schedule

Most job seekers don't have a plan for each week. It is one of the reasons they don't get much done. Follow each of the steps that follow to create your own weekly job search plan. It will make a difference.

Step 1: How Many Hours Per Week?

How many hours per week do you plan to spend looking for a job?

I recommend you spend at least twenty-five hours per week in your job search.

Copyright © 1995 • JIST Works, Inc. • Indianapolis, IN 46202 • (317) 264-3720

Since the average job seeker spends about fifteen hours per week actively looking for work, this is much more than the average. More hours would, of course, be better. Whatever you decide is fine. You should realize that the less time you spend, the longer you are likely to be unemployed.

In the box that follows, write the number of hours per week you plan to spend looking for work.

Number of Hours per Week I Plan on Looking for a Job: _____

Step 2: Which Days of the Week Will You Look?

Decide which days each week you will use to look for work. Since most organizations are open Monday through Friday, these are often the best days to conduct your search. In the first column of the following form, check the days you plan to use for your job search. Don't mark in the other columns yet.

Job Search Days, Hours and Times Worksheet

Days	Number of Hours	Times
____ Sunday	_____	_____ to _____
____ Monday	_____	_____ to _____
____ Tuesday	_____	_____ to _____
____ Wednesday	_____	_____ to _____
____ Thursday	_____	_____ to _____
____ Friday	_____	_____ to _____
____ Saturday	_____	_____ to _____

Total number of hours per week: _____

Copyright © 1995 • JIST Works, Inc. • Indianapolis, IN 46202 • (317) 264-3720

Step 3: How Many Hours Will You Look Each Day?

How many hours will you look for work on each of the days you have selected? Write the number of hours in the second column of the worksheet.

For example, if you selected Mondays, you may decide to spend six hours looking on that day. You would then write "6" in the "Number of Hours" column. Do this with each of the days you checked. Total that column at the bottom of the worksheet. It should equal the number of hours you listed in Step 1.

Step 4: What Times Each Day?

If you plan to look for work for six hours on each Monday, which hours? For example, you may decide to begin at 8:00 a.m. and work until noon (4 hours), take an hour off for lunch, then work from 1:00 p.m. to 3:00 p.m. (2 hours). Complete the third column with this information for each day you selected.

Step 5: Create a Daily Job Search Schedule

Now you have decided which days and hours to spend on your job search. But what will you do each day? You still need a daily plan to get the most out of each hour. Look at the following sample daily schedule. Yours may look different, but you should use many of the same ideas in your own daily schedule.

Sample Daily Schedule

TIME	ACTIVITY
	Morning:
7:00 a.m.	Get up, shower, dress, and eat breakfast *(coffee!!)*
8:00 — 8:15	Organize work space, review schedule for interviews or promised follow ups, update schedule as needed
8:15 — 9:00	Review old leads for follow up *(from follow-up box)*, develop new leads from want ads, *Yellow Pages,* warm contact lists and other sources, complete daily contact list
9:00 — 10:00	Make phone calls and set up interviews
10:00 — 10:15	Take a break
10:15 — 11:00	Make more phone calls
11:00 — 12:00	Send follow-up notes as needed
	Afternoon:
noon — 1:00 p.m.	Lunch break, relax
1:00 — 3:00	Go on interviews, make cold contacts in the field
Evening:	Read job search books, make calls to warm contacts, work on a "better" resume, spend time with friends and family, exercise, relax

Some Tips for Your Own Daily Schedule

Set a Daily Goal for Interviews

I suggest that you set a goal of at least one interview per day. Many people get two interviews per day if they use the techniques I suggest. This one simple idea can make a big difference.

Look at the information that follows to see how meeting a daily interview goal can add up.

Daily Goals Add Up!

1 interview a day = 20 interviews a month
2 interviews a day = 40 interviews a month

Copyright © 1995 • JIST Works, Inc. • Indianapolis, IN 46202 • (317) 264-3720

Compare this to the average job seeker getting fewer than eight interviews a month.

If you get two interviews a day for a month (five-day weeks), that adds up to forty interviews! That is more interviews than the average job seeker gets in four months. And that is one of the reasons why you can get a job in less time.

Remember to think of an interview as seeing people who hire people like you, but don't necessarily have a job opening now. *Don't stop calling until you have met your daily objective!*

Expect to Get Rejected

Most people make ten to fifteen phone calls to get one interview. Most people can make that many calls in an hour, so two hours of calls can result in two interviews. The calls that don't get you an interview are often friendly. So the rejection you experience is really no big deal.

Make Phone Calls, Be Active

You won't get a job by reading job search books or working on your resume. Save those activities for other times. During the day, concentrate on active job search methods.

Stick to Your Schedule

Arrange interviews at times other than those you planned to spend in your job search office. Plan to take care of your personal business after your office hours, too.

Step 6: Create a Weekly Job Search Schedule

You need to put together a weekly job search schedule and stick to it. The best way to do this is to write down your schedule in advance.

The Weekly Job Search Schedule Worksheets that follow will show you how one person created a weekly schedule that was right for him. Consider what you have learned so far when creating your own schedule.

Make several copies of the blank worksheet and use one for each week during your job search. Or you may want to use a schedule book you already use. You also can buy weekly planners at most stationery or department stores. These are great to use in organizing your time. I use mine every day.

Weekly Job Search Schedule Worksheet

		MONDAY	TUESDAY	WEDNESDAY	THURSDAY	FRIDAY
A.M.	6:00					
	6:30	Get up, shower,				
	7:00	eat breakfast				→
	7:30	↓				
	8:00	Get organized.				
	8:30	Gather old and				→
	9:00	new job leads.				
	9:30	↓				
	10:00	Make phone contacts				
	10:30	follow up & get two interviews				→
	11:00	↓				
	11:30	Write/send				→
P.M.	12:00	follow up correspondence				
	12:30	Plan afternoon				→
	1:00	Lunch				→
	1:30				Appt with Lisa at Welch	
	2:00		Leave for		Whitman & Scott	
	2:30		interview		↓	
	3:00		Interview at		Drop by State Employment	Go to printers for resume
	3:30		Fischer Brothers		Office	
	4:00	Work on	→	Make final revisions of	Take resume to	
	4:30	resume		resume Proof Read!	the printers	Afternoon off
	5:00	Review the day!			→	
	5:30					
	6:00	Dinner				→
	6:30					

Copyright © 1995 • JIST Works, Inc. • Indianapolis, IN 46202 • (317) 264-3720

Weekly Job Search Schedule Worksheet

		MONDAY	TUESDAY	WEDNESDAY	THURSDAY	FRIDAY
A.M.	6:00					
	6:30					
	7:00					
	7:30					
	8:00					
	8:30					
	9:00					
	9:30					
	10:00					
	10:30					
	11:00					
	11:30					
P.M.	12:00					
	12:30					
	1:00					
	1:30					
	2:00					
	2:30					
	3:00					
	3:30					
	4:00					
	4:30					
	5:00					
	5:30					
	6:00					
	6:30					

Copyright © 1995 • JIST Works, Inc. • Indianapolis, IN 46202 • (317) 264-3720

Forms and Filing Systems to Help You Organize Your Job Search

This section provides you with special forms and other ways to organize your job search.

Job Lead Cards

By using the job search methods you have learned in this book, you can develop hundreds of contacts. Keeping track of them is more than your memory can handle. Look at the following 3" x 5" card. It shows the kind of information you can keep about each person who helps you in your job search.

Although the card used in this example is specially printed, you can keep the same kind of information on blank 3" x 5" cards. These cards are available at most department and stationery stores.

Plan on using at least a hundred of these cards. Create one card for each person who gives you a referral or is a possible employer. Keep brief notes each time you talk with that person to help you remember important details for your next contact.

A Sample Job Lead Card

ORGANIZATION: Mutual Health Insurance

CONTACT PERSON: Anna Tomey   PHONE: 317-355-0216

SOURCE OF LEAD: Aunt Ruth

NOTES: 4/10 Called. Anna on vacation. Call back 4/15. 4/15 Interview set 4/20 at 1:30. 4/20 Anna showed me around. they use the same computers we used in school! (Friendly people) Sent thank-you note and JIST Card call back 5/1. 5/1 Second interview 5/8 at 9 a.m.!

Copyright © 1995 • JIST Works, Inc. • Indianapolis, IN 46202 • (317) 264-3720

The Follow-Up Box

Most department and stationery stores have small file boxes made to hold 3" x 5" cards. They also have tabbed dividers for these boxes. Buy an inexpensive card file box and enough dividers to set up a box as described here.

Set up a file box divider for each day of the month, numbering them one through thirty-one. Once this has been done, file each completed Job Lead Card under the date you want to follow up on it.

Examples of How You Can Use the Follow-Up Box

Example 1: You get the name of a referral to call, but you can't get to this person right away. You create a Job Lead Card and file it under tomorrow's date.

Example 2: You call someone from a *Yellow Pages* listing, but he is busy this week. He tells you to call back in two weeks. You file his Job Lead Card under the date exactly two weeks in the future.

Example 3: You get an interview with a person who doesn't have any jobs now, but she gives you a name of someone else who might. After you send a thank-you note and JIST Card, you file her Job Lead Card under a date a few weeks in the future.

As you contact more and more people in your job search, the number of cards you file away for future follow up will keep increasing. You will find more and more "new" leads as you follow up with people you've already contacted one or more times in the past. This is one of the most effective ways of getting a job!

At the beginning of each week, you simply review all the Job Lead Cards you filed for that week. On your weekly schedule, list any interviews or follow-up calls you promised to make for a particular time and date.

At the beginning of each day, pull the Job Lead Cards filed under that date. List them on your Daily Contact Sheet *(described in the following section)* for that day.

The Daily Contact Sheet

You can make copies of the form I have provided or make your own on regular lined sheets of paper.

Begin each day by completing one of these forms. I suggest that you list at least twenty people or organizations to contact before you begin any phone calls that day. Use any source to get these leads including people you know, referrals, *Yellow Page* leads, want ads, and any other source.

The sample that follows will give you an idea of how the form works.

Daily Contact Sheet

CONTACT NAME/ORGANIZATION	REFERRAL SOURCE	JOB LEAD CARD	PHONE NUMBER
1. Manager/The Flower Shoppe	Yellow Pages	Yes	897-6041
2. Manager/Rainbow Flowers	Yellow Pages	Yes	897-7365
3. Joyce Wilson/Hartley Nurseries	John Lee	Yes	892-2224
4. John Mullahy/Roses, Etc.	Uncle Jim	Yes	299-4326
5. none/Plants to Go	Want Ad	Yes	835-7016

Daily Contact Sheet

CONTACT NAME/ORGANIZATION	REFERRAL SOURCE	JOB LEAD CARD	PHONE NUMBER
1.			
2.			
3.			
4.			
5.			
6.			
7.			
8.			
9.			
10.			
11.			
12.			
13.			
14.			
15.			
16.			
17.			
18.			
19.			
20.			

Copyright © 1995 • JIST Works, Inc. • Indianapolis, IN 46202 • (317) 264-3720

A Few Final Words on Being Organized

Most people don't find the job search to be a fun experience. There is lots of rejection involved. To avoid failure, they find lots of ways to avoid looking for work.

Of course, delaying your job search just leaves you unemployed longer than you need to be. So don't get discouraged. The best way to shorten your job search is to structure your time as if your job search is your job.

Looking for a job is hard work, so take time for breaks. And take time to take care of yourself. Someone out there needs you — and will be happy to have you.

Copyright © 1995 • JIST Works, Inc. • Indianapolis, IN 46202 • (317) 264-3720

Surviving on a New Job

And Some Tips on Getting Ahead

Most of this book has been about getting a job. This chapter is about keeping it — and getting ahead.

During the years you work you are likely to have many different jobs. Each one will present chances to learn and problems to overcome.

As you begin a new job, you will probably feel a bit of fear. Often, you don't know what to expect:

- Will you get along with the other people who work there?
- Are you dressed right?
- Will you be able to handle the new responsibilities?

Copyright © 1995 • JIST Works, Inc. • Indianapolis, IN 46202 • (317) 264-3720

These and other concerns will be on your mind as you begin a new job. This chapter can help you get off to a successful start. You also will find important information on how to get ahead once you are on the job.

Surviving on the Job

There are things you can do to increase your chances of success on a new job. If you want to do well, you may need to change the way you act, and some of your attitudes.

 Surveys of employers indicate the major reasons why a person does not do well on the job. Look at the following list of reasons why people have been fired. Check the top three reasons you think employers gave for firing an employee.

Why People Get Fired

_____	Unable to get along with other workers
_____	Was dishonest (lied or stole things)
_____	Poor dress or grooming
_____	Unreliable, too many days absent or late
_____	Used work time for personal business
_____	Couldn't do the work
_____	Worked too slowly, made too many mistakes
_____	Would not follow orders, did not get along with supervisor
_____	Abused alcohol or drugs
_____	Misrepresented their skills or experience
_____	Too many accidents, did not follow safety rules

A Review of the Reasons People Are Fired

Let's review each of the major reasons for being fired. Check your top three reasons against what employers actually said.

Unable to Get Along with Other Workers

Employers do not give this as one of the top three reasons for firing someone. But workers consider this problem one of the top reasons they don't like their jobs. Many people leave their jobs because they don't like the people they work with. Not getting along also probably would affect your productivity on the job.

Copyright © 1995 • JIST Works, Inc. • Indianapolis, IN 46202 • (317) 264-3720

Dishonesty

This is one of the top reasons employers give for firing someone. Employers don't want to pay someone who steals from them or can't be trusted. More employers are now screening new applicants to eliminate people who have been dishonest with previous employers.

Poor Dress or Grooming

The way you look is very important. This is particularly true in office jobs and in jobs where you deal with customers. Employers don't give this as a top reason for firing someone, but it can affect how they feel about someone. For example, someone with poor dress or grooming may not be given more responsibility.

Unreliable, Too Many Days Absent or Late

When an employee is absent, it disrupts the work of other people. Coworkers may have to neglect their work to make up for the absent worker. Now two or more people are behind in their work. People who are often late also set a bad example for others. Employers place these problems high on their list of reasons for firing people.

Couldn't Do the Work

Few people get fired because they could not do the work. Employers tend to hire people they think can do the job, and then give them time to learn it.

Worked Too Slowly, Made Too Many Mistakes

This is one of the top three reasons employers give for firing people. You can see why: unproductive employees cost more than they earn! A slow worker is expensive compared to another worker who gets the same job done in less time. A slow worker also can slow down the work of coworkers or cause resentment from others who feel they are working harder.

Workers who make mistakes also can be costly in many ways. Perhaps another employee has to spend time correcting errors. A customer may become dissatisfied with the company's products or services as a result of sloppy work. That customer doesn't come back — and tells others not to!

Would Not Follow Orders, Did Not Get Along with Supervisor

In a disagreement with a supervisor, you will almost always lose! In fact, this is one of the top three reasons people get fired.

Abuse of Alcohol or Drugs

Substance abuse has become a major problem, but it is not among the top three reasons for being fired. This may be because a person who abuses alcohol or drugs gets fired for being unreliable, or some other reason. The employer may not even know the cause of the problem.

Copyright © 1995 • JIST Works, Inc. • Indianapolis, IN 46202 • (317) 264-3720

Too Many Accidents, Did Not Follow Safety Rules

Employers do not want to employ people who have "accidents" or who do not follow safety rules. Accidents can be costly to employers and to other employees. Fortunately, most people follow good safety rules. This is not among the top reasons employers give for firing people.

More Reasons

There are many reasons an employer might fire someone. Almost any reason can be enough if it is a serious problem. More often, however, people are fired for more than one reason. For example, they may be late to work too often and make too many mistakes in their work. Or they do not get along with their supervisor and don't get enough done.

 In the following spaces, list at least three other reasons an employer might have to fire someone. Perhaps you know someone who was fired. Or can think of a reason you might fire someone.

1. _____
   _____
2. _____
   _____
3. _____
   _____

Tips for Getting Off to a Good Start on a New Job

Now you know why most people get fired. But that doesn't tell you what you can do to be successful on a new job. This section provides tips to help you get started and succeed in a new job.

As you read these suggestions, use the space below each tip to write notes about how you could use each one. Sample notes are provided for the first few tips to give you ideas. Use extra paper if you need more space for your notes.

Basic Things You Should Do — And Not Do on the Job

Following are some basic tips for getting along on a new job. Some of them have to do with your attitude toward your job and the people you work with.

Copyright © 1995 • JIST Works, Inc. • Indianapolis, IN 46202 • (317) 264-3720

There Is No Such Thing as a "Dead-End Job"

Learn all you can from any job you have. Do it as well as you are able. Look for chances to put your skills to better use. Even if you are not able to move up in this organization, a "dead-end" job can give you a good reference for a different position.

One Person's Notes in Response to This Item:

1. If I can't get my ideal job, then I'll settle for a job that lets me use most of the skills I want to develop. Also, I want to get more experience in the same industry. I see myself as long-term — even if I have to start at the bottom.

2. Let the boss and personnel department know that I am taking extra classes at night — and that I hope to move up within the company when I am finished.

 Write your own notes here:

1. _____

2. _____

3. _____

4. _____

5. _____

Don't Miss Work

A minor illness, like a cold, is not a good reason for missing work. Nor are most personal problems such as child care or getting your car fixed. If you miss more than three days a year for these reasons, it may be too much. Using "sick" time for personal reasons is dishonest. Even if you don't feel well, using too much sick time can call attention to yourself in a negative way. A new employee cannot afford this kind of attention.

Copyright © 1995 • JIST Works, Inc. • Indianapolis, IN 46202 • (317) 264-3720

One Person's Notes in Response to This Item:

1. <u>I need to set up better ways of handling my personal business after work</u>
   <u>hours and on weekends. I will arrange for a ride with a coworker for those</u>
   <u>days when I have car problems.</u>
2. <u>I will try to have no absences at all during my first year on the job.</u>

 Write your own notes here:

1. _____
   _____
2. _____
   _____
3. _____
   _____
4. _____
   _____
5. _____
   _____

Be on Time

There are very few acceptable reasons for being late. Usually, being late is your own fault and could be avoided. For example, "I missed the bus," and "I ran out of gas" are poor excuses. You could easily have avoided either problem. Identify the reasons you are most likely to be late and eliminate them.

 Write your own notes here:

1. _____
   _____
2. _____
   _____
3. _____
   _____

190

Copyright © 1995 • JIST Works, Inc. • Indianapolis, IN 46202 • (317) 264-3720

4. _____

5. _____

Call If You Will Be Absent or Late

If you will be more than a few minutes late or absent for any reason, call in at the beginning of the work day. Talk directly to your supervisor and explain the situation. Do not leave a message. Sometimes, you may be able to call the day before if you think there could be a problem.

Write your own notes here:

1. _____

2. _____

3. _____

4. _____

5. _____

Be Neat and Clean

Be careful about your grooming. Be aware of how you look at all times. It is important that your clothes fit well, are clean, and look good. Notice how others dress in jobs similar to yours. Dress at least as well, but cleaner. Write some ideas about the clothes you have that you can wear on the job. Wear these outfits and ask others how you look.

Copyright © 1995 • JIST Works, Inc. • Indianapolis, IN 46202 • (317) 264-3720

Write your own notes here:

1. _____
_____
2. _____
_____
3. _____
_____
4. _____
_____
5. _____
_____

Find a "Buddy" to Help You

New employees are often assigned a coworker to teach them the basics of the job. If you are not assigned someone like this, find your own. After you are there a few days, look for someone you think you will get along with, and knows the work. Ask him or her to help you out. Go out of your way to be nice to this person.

Write your own notes here:

1. _____
_____
2. _____
_____
3. _____
_____
4. _____
_____
5. _____
_____

Read Personnel and Procedure Manuals

Most larger organizations have manuals that give the office rules and instructions for doing various parts of the job. Ask your supervisor for these and read

Copyright © 1995 • JIST Works, Inc. • Indianapolis, IN 46202 • (317) 264-3720

them as soon as possible. Many smaller organizations will not have these manuals. You will need to ask your supervisor to explain any special procedures or rules to you.

 Write your own notes here:

1. _____
   _____
2. _____
   _____
3. _____
   _____
4. _____
   _____
5. _____
   _____

Stay Away from *Problem* Employees

There are always some negative and complaining people in any workplace. Others do things against the rules, waste time, or are not good workers in other ways. They may be fun to be with. But spending time with them will affect your job. Your coworkers and supervisors may begin to see you as a "problem." Be friendly. But do not socialize with people like this any more than necessary.

 Write your own notes here:

1. _____
   _____
2. _____
   _____
3. _____
   _____
4. _____
   _____
5. _____
   _____

Copyright © 1995 • JIST Works, Inc. • Indianapolis, IN 46202 • (317) 264-3720

Keep Personal Problems at Home

You are paid to get a job done. Do not spend time on personal concerns if you can avoid it. Making personal phone calls, paying bills, coming back late from lunch, talking to other staff about what you did last weekend, or getting to work late for any reason, is not what you are being paid to do.

Although some socializing on the job is common, you can easily overdo it. Limit your personal activities and discussions to breaks, lunch times, or hours outside of work as much as possible.

 Write your own notes here:

1. _____
   _____
2. _____
   _____
3. _____
   _____
4. _____
   _____
5. _____
   _____

Keep Children at Home Too

They may be the most important part of your life, but child care is not the concern of an employer. If you expect to work full time, you must find ways to separate family responsibilities from your role as an employee. Arrange child care so that you do not miss work when they are ill. Strongly discourage phone calls to or from children except in emergencies. When interviewing for a job, tell employers that you will be a dependable worker and that child care has been arranged. Assure them that you needn't miss work for this reason — then make sure you don't.

Copyright © 1995 • JIST Works, Inc. • Indianapolis, IN 46202 • (317) 264-3720

Write your own notes here:

1. _____
   _____
2. _____
   _____
3. _____
   _____
4. _____
   _____
5. _____
   _____

Work Fast, But Carefully

It is important to work at a steady and quick pace. Find a pace that you can keep up all day without making errors. Correcting mistakes just wastes time later. This way of working requires concentration. You will need to make good use of breaks and lunch periods for rest.

Write your own notes here:

1. _____
   _____
2. _____
   _____
3. _____
   _____
4. _____
   _____
5. _____
   _____

Copyright © 1995 • JIST Works, Inc. • Indianapolis, IN 46202 • (317) 264-3720

Advanced Tips — Extra Things You Can Do to Get Ahead

Following the basic tips presented in the previous section can help you get off to a good start. If you want to be promoted or have more control over what you do on your job, there are additional things you can do. Doing these things will help you get positive attention. They also can help you get promotions and performance increases. Of course, your work will have to be good as well. There are no guarantees of success, but these tips will help.

As before, use the space following each tip to write notes on how you can best apply it to your own situation.

Dress and Groom for a Promotion

If you want to get ahead in an organization, dress and groom as if you work at the level you hope to reach next. This is not always possible, but at the very least, be clean and well-groomed. Wear clothes that fit well and look good on you. Copy the clothing styles of others in the organization who are successful. Even when your coworkers see you away from work, present the image you want for yourself at work.

 Write your own notes here:

1. _____
_____
2. _____
_____
3. _____
_____
4. _____
_____
5. _____
_____

Be Early and Stay Late

Get to work early each day. Use this time to list what you plan to get done that day. At the end of the day, leave at least a few minutes after quitting time. Let the boss know that you are willing to stay late to meet an important deadline. If you do stay late, let the boss know!

Some employers may not want you to work beyond your regular hours. They fear problems with governmental agencies that may force them to pay overtime

Copyright © 1995 • JIST Works, Inc. • Indianapolis, IN 46202 • (317) 264-3720

wages. If this is so, do what your employer wants you to do, but make it clear that you are willing to help in any way needed.

 Write your own notes here:

1. _____

2. _____

3. _____

4. _____

5. _____

Be Enthusiastic

Go out of your way to find ways to enjoy your job. Tell others what you like about it, particularly those you work with. Emphasize those parts of your job that you like to do and do well. Share this enthusiasm even in conversations with your friends. Go out of your way to tell your supervisor what you like about your job. This will help you focus on the parts of your job you do best and want to develop. It also will help others notice that you do those things well.

 Write your own notes here:

1. _____

2. _____

3. _____

4. _____

5. _____

Copyright © 1995 • JIST Works, Inc. • Indianapolis, IN 46202 • (317) 264-3720

Ask for More Responsibility

Be willing to take on more responsibility. Let the boss know you want to move up. As soon as you begin a new job, look for ways to learn new things. Volunteer to help out in ways you feel will make you more valuable to the organization. And ask for advice about what you can do to be more valuable to the organization.

 Write your own notes here:

1. _____
   _____
2. _____
   _____
3. _____
   _____
4. _____
   _____
5. _____
   _____

Ask How You Can Earn More Money

In your first week on the job, ask your supervisor to see you for about thirty minutes of private time. When you have his or her attention, say that you want to be more valuable to the organization. Ask what you can do to get a raise within a reasonable amount of time. Request special assignments to help develop your skills.

Before you leave, ask for a specific future date to go over your progress. Make sure you know what you have to do to get the raise. Ask the boss to give you feedback on your progress from time to time.

 Write your own notes here:

1. _____
   _____
2. _____
   _____

Copyright © 1995 • JIST Works, Inc. • Indianapolis, IN 46202 • (317) 264-3720

3. _____
_____
4. _____
_____
5. _____
_____

Ask for Training

Get as much training as possible! Take any training that is available from your employer. Even if it is not in your area of responsibility, it may help you gain new skills in other areas. Define what training you need to do your job better. If it is not available through your employer, explain to your supervisor how the training will help the organization. Ask for help in finding the best training source.

Write your own notes here:

1. _____
_____
2. _____
_____
3. _____
_____
4. _____
_____
5. _____
_____

Learn on Your Own Time

Decide what you need to learn to get ahead — or to get the job you want. Take evening classes. Instead of watching TV at home, read books and magazines on related subjects. Stay up with what is going on in your field.

Computer skills and the use of new technologies are very important. If your job does not require you to develop these skills, it is most important that you go out and learn them outside of your job. Then look for ways to use these new technologies and skills in your present job.

Write your own notes here:

1. _____
   _____
2. _____
   _____
3. _____
   _____
4. _____
   _____
5. _____
   _____

Take on Difficult Projects

You won't get much positive attention unless you do more than is expected of you. Look for projects you think you can do well, and would benefit the organization in some clear way. Don't promise too much, and keep a low profile while you do the work. If no one expects too much, it is easier to be seen as successful, even if your results are not as good as you had hoped.

Write your own notes here:

1. _____
   _____
2. _____
   _____
3. _____
   _____
4. _____
   _____
5. _____
   _____

Copyright © 1995 • JIST Works, Inc. • Indianapolis, IN 46202 • (317) 264-3720

Get Measurable Results

Look for some way to measure the results of your work. Keep records of what you do. Compare your results to past performance or the average performance of others in similar situations. If your results look good, send a report to your supervisor. For example, if the number of orders went up 40 percent over the same month last year with no increase in staff, that's a big accomplishment.

Look for Ways to Present What You Do in Numbers

- Dollars saved
- Percent of increased sales
- Number of persons served
- Number of units processed
- Size of budget

Write your own notes here:

1. _____
   _____
2. _____
   _____
3. _____
   _____
4. _____
   _____
5. _____
   _____

Don't Just Quit

Sometimes a job just doesn't work out. Maybe you feel that you won't get ahead there. It is often better to begin looking for another job than to allow yourself to get negative. But ask for a job change within the organization before you give up. Or be more assertive in asking your boss for more responsibility or different assignments.

If you do decide to leave, begin looking for a job but don't share this with coworkers. Make every effort to do your job and be positive. When you find another job, give thirty days notice if at all possible. Remember that your next

Copyright © 1995 • JIST Works, Inc. • Indianapolis, IN 46202 • (317) 264-3720

employer will want to contact your previous ones, so do be as friendly and as productive as possible in your final days.

 Write your own notes here:

1. _____

_____

2. _____

_____

3. _____

_____

4. _____

_____

5. _____

_____

And Now, in Conclusion . . .

This book now comes to an end. But, for you, there is so much more to come. The final lessons I can offer are these:

✔ Trust yourself. No one can know you better than you.

✔ Decide to do something worthwhile. Whether it is raising a family or saving the whales, believe in something you do as special, as lasting, as valuable.

✔ Work well. All work is worth doing, so put your energy into it and do it as well as you are able.

✔ Enjoy life. It's sort of the same as having fun, but lasts longer and means more.

✔ Send thank-you notes. Many people will help you throughout your life, in large and small ways. Let them know you appreciate them. The more you give, the more you seem to get in return.

Thank you for reading this book. I wish you good fortune in your job search and your life.

Copyright © 1995 • JIST Works, Inc. • Indianapolis, IN 46202 • (317) 264-3720

THE QUICK RESUME and COVER LETTER BOOK

Write and Use an Effective Resume is Only One Day

By J. Michael Farr

First title in JIST's new Quick Guides series, by a best-selling author whose job search books have sold more than one million copies! Contains an "Instant Resume Worksheet" that enables job seekers to put together a basic, acceptable resume in less than one day. Provides helpful advice on creating job objectives, identifying skills, dealing with special situations, and getting a job.

OTHER INFORMATION
- Logical structure makes information easy to locate
- Contains more than 50 sample resumes and cover letters
- Crucial career planning and job search sections

> 7 x 9, Paper, 288 pp.
> **ISBN 1-56370-141-3**
> **$9.95**   Order Code RCLQG

THE QUICK INTERVIEW and SALARY NEGOTIATION BOOK

Dramatically Improve Your Interviewing Skill — and Pay — in a Matter of Hours

By J. Michael Farr

New, second title of JIST's Quick Guide Series. J. Michael Farr's career books have sold more than 1 million copies. He has taught job search methods to trainers and instructors for nearly 20 years. In this informative book, he shares successful interview and salary negotiation techniques that have helped thousands find jobs and get better salaries.

OTHER INFORMATION
- Outlines the three most important things to do in an interview
- Details how to make a $1,000 per minute in your negotiations
- Explains how to answer key problem questions

> 7 x 9, Paper, 220 pp.
> **ISBN 1-56370-162-6**
> **$9.95**   Order Code J1626

GALLERY of BEST RESUMES

A Collection of Quality Resumes by Professional Resume Writers

By David F. Noble

A showcase collection of quality resumes for seeking a job or changing career. Contains outstanding examples of different types of resumes for a variety of occupations grouped by category, such as Accounting/Finance, Administrative Assistance/Secretary, Graduating/Graduated Student, Management, etc. Includes helpful tips and techniques consistently used in the best resumes. A set of sample resumes printed on high-quality paper stock is bound right into the book.

OTHER INFORMATION
- Contains more than 200 resumes and 25 companion cover letters written by members of the Professional Association of Resume Writers
- 101 best resume tips
- 30 tips for polishing cover letters

> 8 1/2 x 11, Paper, 400 pp.
> **ISBN 1-56370-144-8**
> **$16.95**   Order Code GBR

*Look for these and other fine books from JIST Works, Inc., at your full service bookstore
or call us for additional information.*

THE OCCUPATIONAL OUTLOOK HANDBOOK 1994-1995 Edition

By U.S. Department of Labor

This low-cost JIST edition of the U.S Department of Labor's popular career exploration guide describes the 250 jobs in which 85% of the American workforce is employed. Valuable information about each occupation includes a description of the work itself, employment outlook and opportunities, earnings, related occupations, training and advancement, and sources of additional information.

OTHER INFORMATION

- The standard career reference book
- The most widely used and known career reference for professionals and schools
- Includes the latest Department of Labor statistics

8 1/2 x 11, Paper, 544 pp.	8 1/2 x 11, Hardback, 544 pp.
ISBN 1-56370-160-X	**ISBN 1-56370-161-X**
$15.95 Order Code OOH4	**$21.95** Order Code OOHH4

AMERICA'S TOP 300 JOBS — 4th Edition

A Complete Career Handbook

Praised by job search professionals as the most authoritative book of its kind on current and emerging jobs of the 1990s, it provides detailed descriptions of the 250 jobs in which more than 85 percent of the workforce are employed. Also includes information on more than 70 additional jobs.

OTHER INFORMATION

- Completely revised content
- The latest trends and salary projections based on U.S Department of Labor information

8 1/2 x 11, Paper, 544 pp.
ISBN 1-56370-163-4
$17.95 Order Code T3004

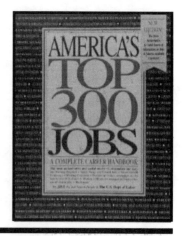

AMERICA'S 50 FASTEST GROWING JOBS — 2nd Edition

The Authoritative Information Source

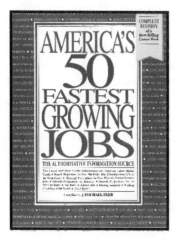

This best-selling career book contains detailed job descriptions for the 50 fastest-growing occupations. Tables list the fastest-growing jobs, which include paralegals, medical assistants, physical therapists, computer repair technicians, and pilots. Also includes information about related occupations for each of the fastest-growing jobs, a job search section, and details on more than 500 jobs.

OTHER INFORMATION

- Contains information about related occupations for each of the fastest growing jobs
- A job search section
- Details for than 500 jobs

8 1/2 x 11, Paper, 201 pp.
ISBN 1-56370-091-3
$11.95 Order Code AFF

Look for these and other fine books from JIST Works, Inc., at your full service bookstore or call us for additional information.